What People Are Saying About
Brigantia: Warrior Goddess

A deeply researched book, that, while acknowledging Brigantia's later imperial associations, digs far beneath them to uncover the deep roots of a complex and multi-faceted goddess, and offers ways to work with her symbols today. I learned so much reading this. A fascinating work. The authors dedication to her subject shines.
Kelle Bandea, D.Min., Author of *Modron; Meeting the Celtic Mother Goddess*

Pauline Breen seamlessly blends scholarship with spirituality in this potent examination of Brigantia. Nothing exists within the vacuum, and the historical and cultural background provide a contextual foundation that is crucial in working with such deities (or aspects of deities) that are not as well known or whose worship has not been popularized. In reading this work, I feel like I not only joyfully travelled through time but I was able to meet and connect with Brigantia on a personal level. This book is engaging and however you want to integrate Brigantia's power and wisdom into your life, this is the perfect guide to start and a way to learn the broader historical influence of one of the most interesting and influential times in Western history.
Mark NeCamp, Jr., Author of *Energy Magick*

Pagan Portals
Brigantia

Warrior Goddess

Pagan Portals
Brigantia

Warrior Goddess

Pauline Breen

MOON
BOOKS

London, UK
Washington, DC, USA

First published by Moon Books, 2025
Moon Books is an imprint of Collective Ink Ltd.,
Unit 11, Shepperton House, 89 Shepperton Road, London, N1 3DF
office@collectiveinkbooks.com
www.collectiveinkbooks.com
www.moon-books.net

For distributor details and how to order please visit the 'Ordering' section on our website.

Text copyright: Pauline Breen 2024

ISBN: 978 1 80341 874 2
978 1 80341 875 9 (ebook)
Library of Congress Control Number: 2024938134

All rights reserved. Except for brief quotations in critical articles or reviews, no part of this book may be reproduced in any manner without prior written permission from the publishers.

The rights of Pauline Breen as author have been asserted in accordance with the Copyright, Designs and Patents Act 1988.

A CIP catalogue record for this book is available from the British Library.

Design: Lapiz Digital Services

UK: Printed and bound by CPI Group (UK) Ltd, Croydon, CR0 4YY
Printed in North America by CPI GPS partners

We operate a distinctive and ethical publishing philosophy in all areas of our business, from our global network of authors to production and worldwide distribution.

Contents

Introduction	ix
Chapter 1 Pre-Roman and Roman Britain	1
British Celts	1
Roman Invasion	6
Chapter 2 War, Death and the Celts	15
The Celts and War	15
The Influence of Gaul	17
Celtic Women and War	18
Boudicca	20
Celtic Deities	22
Chapter 3 Brigantia	24
Brigantia	24
Roman Inscriptions of Britain	27
The Brigantes	35
Brig	40
Jupiter	43
Caelestis of Carthage	43
Minerva	45
Brigantia and Brigid of Ireland	47
Influence of Other Classical Deities	48
Chapter 4 Connecting with Brigantia	52
Journey to Hadrian's Wall	52
Animals	54
Colours	59
Symbols of Brigantia	60
Chapter 5 What Does Brigantia Stand For?	66
Conclusion	71
Bibliography	77
About the Author	82

For Brigid

Introduction

When I first felt drawn to writing about Brigid, I knew that I would write three non-fiction books about her. Perhaps it was the magic of the number three so prevalent in the Celtic culture or maybe it was indicative of my ever-growing relationship with the remarkable goddess Brigid that would push me to research her in as much detail as possible for my own benefit firstly, then share my findings with all those who also had an interest in her. Each book has so far been a journey and a half that leaves me more enthralled with Brigid and wanting to know even more about her. Each face of Brigid that I am drawn to and discover is profound and precise. Each version of Brigid reveals herself to be a particular energy to whom I can turn, for specific assistance or veneration. Discovering and working with Brigantia has been no different. Getting to know Brigantia has completed my personal triad of Brigid.

Brigit has always been considered a triple goddess of healing, poetry and smithcraft. Within the goddess I see two more very distinctive personas who have all contributed significantly to my own journey with the sacred divine feminine. The Goddess Brigit brought remembrance to me; remembrance of the divine feminine. Maman Brigitte brought authenticity to me that only the Dark Goddess can bring and for the last leg of my research journey I meet Brigantia who brings empowerment to the table. In my opinion the three sides of her are interconnected, ever flowing and mutually responsible to reinforce the existence and power of each other. These three 'Brigids', in my opinion, exist within her, within the one Brigid.

The order of their appearances in my life have mirrored my internal growth to my external experiences. Brigit, Maman Brigitte and Brigantia have been sequential in their revelation to me. I believe the dark work facilitated by Brigitte could only come from a place of safety and sanctity provided by my relationship to the Goddess Brigit, and I believe the state of empowerment from Brigantia can only be genuinely effective if the journey to the shadow with Maman Brigitte has been undertaken. This may not be the case for everybody, but it certainly was for me.

Who is Brigantia? Brigantia is, in my opinion, a proto-Brigid. I believe the goddess came in with the Brigantes tribe into the southeast of Ireland and from there she went through a cultural transformation and rebirthed into Brigit the goddess and later Saint Brigid. This is my opinion, of course, and nothing can be one hundred per cent verified but I believe there is ample evidence to give this possibility serious consideration.

Brigantia trips off the tongue in a European pronounced manner that feels quite Hispanic to me and yet, it would appear that she is most probably a Celtic goddess, a British Celtic goddess to be precise. She may in fact also be Roman or indeed a blend of both. I have always felt Brigid to be a blend of energy and this is what makes her unique. As a blend, Brigantia is no different it seems. Brigid is a blend of Goddess and Saint. Maman Brigitte is a blend of Brigid of Ireland and Oya of Africa. And Brigantia is a blend of Gaul, of the Celtic race and one of the greatest civilisations, perhaps of all time, Rome. These origins in Brigantia are already setting quite the scene.

Brigid is a blended, fused energy, of worlds that at first glance appear immiscible but in actual fact are quite integrable. These fusion of energies are evident with the blending of the pagan and Christian world from goddess to Saint as Brigid and also with Ireland, Africa and Haiti as Maman Brigitte. Maybe this blend began with Brigantia. Gaulish migration into Britain brought the Celtic goddess and Roman presence in Britain, would have a monumental impact on us even encountering Brigantia. If it weren't for the literacy and craftmanship of the Romans, we would not have read of Brigantia on inscriptions which is from where we get the majority of our information about Brigantia. Brigantia, may have been venerated in Celtic Britain before the arrival of the Romans but we have no way of knowing that for sure. One thing is for certain, is that her name was spoken and written whilst the Romans occupied Britain, and as such, Brigantia, under Roman rule flourished. What was most important to the Romans was war. Warrior values were thus placed onto Brigantia, equating her with other classical war goddesses of her time such as Athena, but mostly Minerva. Again, we have no way of knowing if Brigantia was associated with war before Roman arrival but within this warrior context, epigraphic evidence tells us of her prestige in Celtic Britain, which coincided with Roman occupation.

Perhaps Brigantia was a deliberate creation of Rome in an attempt to move away from the female mother goddess representation of old Europe to a patriarchy where warrior values would dominate. Maybe she was intentionally fabricated by the Romans to possibly portray female participation in the birthing of a new world. It could be that a goddess with warring characteristics was the perfect female, in imperial eyes. Maybe these warring values were already found in the pre-existing Brigantia of Briton onto which the Roman Brigantia could be superimposed. This is where I consider the blend that I most associate with Brigid to have started, right here with Brigantia. Just like Brigid who could straddle two eras and two worlds of Paganism and Christianity, like Maman Brigitte who could merge African traditional religions to Christianity, Brigantia had the same capacity to bridge worlds. As the old matrifocal world was fused with the new patriarchal world, Brigantia stood present with one foot in each world. As such, she holds the space of classical and Celtic, matrifocal and patriarchal, new and old, and could be considered the quintessential balance of female and male energy.

What I find fascinating is that once Roman troops left Britain, there is little to no mention of Brigantia. This could indicate that she was indeed a creation of Rome, or it could indicate that despite the blend of matrifocal and patriarchal within Brigantia, she evolved and rebirthed across the Atlantic in Ireland (Goddess and Saint), through the incoming Brigantes tribes and overseas in America (Maman Brigitte) through Irish immigrants. We could either view this as her refusal to be associated with patriarchal values and as such subdivides and becomes what is needed by her people, for her people. Or we can view her as maintaining war like tendencies that were either not needed in her new forms, or not encouraged. If we do consider Brigantia, a war goddess, as a proto-Brigid, we can see how the theme of war featured somewhat, not at all, or considerably in the various other personas of Brigid that may have come from Brigantia. Brigit as goddess was eternal defender of the people of Leinster, the Laigin. It is said that she terrified their enemies in the same manner as the war-goddesses Macha, Badb and the Morrigan (Byrne, 1973). She has direct associations with the military base at the Curragh, Kildare and is also, in typical Brigit essence, Brig ambue, the goddess of warriors without status. Brigid as Saint vehemently opposed all aspects of war. Under the Christian light she was peacemaker and went out of her way to avoid war. The tree under which the Saint built her first oratory was held with such sanctity that it never came into contact with a weapon of war (Condren, 1989). Maman Brigitte was birthed during enforced slavery in Haiti which led to the Haitian revolution. She rose to prominence with the emigration of Haitians and the Irish in the American South. In societies where war was notable feature of everyday life or something to be avoided at all costs, the warring attributes within Brigid were either venerated or ignored. If we understand the origins of Brigantia we cannot but associate her with war. Rather than shun this part of her we can view Brigantia as a face of Brigid who presides over all issues pertaining to combat. As such, she can be a powerful

Introduction

figure to provide solace, comfort or inspiration for action. To ignore this facet of her is, in my opinion, to deny her in all her forms. Brigantia can be a powerful patroness for all those living through and affected by war. She can also be hope that just as she rebirthed into Goddess, Saint and Dark goddess she will continue to blend and be that ever expanding, transmuting energy that overcomes all adversity.

The book will endeavour to explore Brigantia's origins based on evidence available to us. This evidence is mostly linguistic and is mainly through the Roman Inscriptions of Britain that will be examined in Chapter 3. Evidence for Brigantia is scant to say the least but it is sufficient, I think, to join the dots and detect a specific personality of Brigid who, as Brigantia, may be justly considered a warrior goddess.

From my research I discovered that Brigantia was a sacred deity to both the warring Celts as well as the Romans, specifically during the rule of Emperor Severus. She was the goddess of the land in both Celtic and Roman cultures. For these reasons, I strongly associate her with the element of earth. For the British Celts she was the goddess of the Brigantes, a tribe of the north and was the name used by the Romans to rename the lands of Britannia. In her most primal earthly association, I sense a wild woman energy with Brigantia. As a deity of the land, I regard her a tribal, territorial goddess. I also deem her energy *as* the land. She is of the trees, crystals, mountain tops, hill tops, groves, bushes and plants. If I were to give her an image, I imagine her to wear the fur of the hunt around her shoulders and her head to be adorned with antlers. I envision Brigantia to have the unmistakable flaming red hair associated with Brigid and it is as wild and messy as can be. On her face, I imagine blue paint, smeared and revealing of her wild, vivacious personality. This is, however, but one aspect of her persona. It is the part that is Gaulish and British Celtic. But she is more than that. She is also imperial.

In her Roman capacity we meet a classical deity. One who is wise, confident and noble but can easily declare war. For the Romans, Brigantia was equated with victory over new lands conquered. Immediately as her name covers firstly a tribe, the Brigantes, and then the entire nation, Britannia, we can instantly see a surge in her power and status, made possible, perhaps because of the Roman spotlight on her. Her greatness from regional to national goddess is possibly indicative of her expansive and ever-growing power at the hands of the Romans or demonstrative to the people, that under Roman rule, they too could evolve, grow, and prosper.

Brigantia as goddess of the land to both Celtic and Roman cults may indeed stem from the manifestation of the great mother goddess brought into Britain through the Belgae, Goidels and the Gauls. Her mother goddess energy may also have come with the Romans through Isis who had been assimilated into Roman culture. Regardless of the mother goddess origins, Brigantia, as a mother goddess figure was common to both cults, and her identity as such was closely connected to the land.

Even though we have similarities between Britain and Rome, we can see the differences between Celtic and classical. The first difference contained within Brigantia is the existence of a mother and war goddess. The two may at first seem contradictory or at odds with each other but in fact, it is the same maternal energy that supports as well as defends. As we will later see, the energy of Brigantia contains the maternal and the military. They are fused together from two separate cults that inflate her and project her forward to give us the powerful archetype of warrior queen, defender and slayer of all that she loves to the nth degree. Brigantia, belonging to two worlds is the balance of both worlds of female and male energy. She is giver and taker, nurturer and defender, creator and destroyer. As mother goddess she is the birther of humanity and as war goddess she is the force of continued life for the tribe, nation and Earth which was important for both the Celts and the Romans. She shows us with confidence, that she is, in addition to the bountiful, abundant mother goddess, that she is the reactive, defensive, territorial goddess that will not stay quiet or stay seated when her boundaries are pushed.

In my opinion, Brigantia is the guise of Brigid that represents authority. She embodies strength, courage, fierceness and action. This authority is a powerful archetype of Brigid available to us all. Although she is available for us in any part of our lives, I feel her energy is more palpable in our queen years, when we're mature and have the time to focus on ourselves and we're ready to step into our power. Or when we arrive at a certain age and we know time is ticking by, so if not now, when? This regal sense of Brigantia is compounded, for me, by her historical link to the female leader of the Brigantian tribe, Queen Cartimandua. I also get a sense of queenliness from her as she is a deity I associate with rising to action, gathering her troops and getting things done. Such dedication to a cause comes from a deep sense of knowing the self and eagerness to fulfil one's purpose that comes rushing forth with age and wisdom. As Queen, she has gone past the mothering or ability to mother stage of her life and is not quite yet the Crone. In between these stages of life, we find the queen years. Brigantia is now the queen of her life, the queen of the Brigantes and queen of the land. As such, she is the perfect queen model.

I also sense her as a tall, royal, authoritative figure that appears out of the mists as a regal, otherworldly figure. I sense her dressed in royal blue with shimmering gold, wearing a crown and observing intently before deciding on the best course of action. She is gracious, grounded and in command.

If I were to sum up Brigantia I would say that she is a universal deity spread out across the pagan Celtic world with Indo-European origins and with significant Roman and Greek sway. The abovementioned blend is perhaps too weak to convey the multiple influences that took an effect on her. We're talking about Celtic influences that were influenced by the Near East and we're talking about Roman influence who themselves were influenced by the Etruscans, the Greeks, Africa and the East.

With such specific resources available to her from the plethora of deities from various cultures she is the chosen one to be the tribal protector of her tribe and their land. From the Roman side she is blended from the supreme power of Jupiter, celestial energies of Caelestis of Carthage (Africa) as well as the warring energies of Minerva. From Jupiter she may take his supreme omnipotence. From Caelestis she may also be considered a sky goddess. From Minerva she may take her strategic planning and organisation.

From the Celtic side I feel her to be the mother goddess who has grown into a sovereign queen energy. She is the raw, natural energies of the land. She is the decisiveness of Queen Cartimandua to march to the beat of her own drum who caused much stir by divorcing her husband. She also runs through the veins of fearless Celtic Women such as Boudicca who rallied troops to avenge the rape of her daughters.

To both cultures she is the protector of the tribe, defender of the enemy and the goddess and guardian of soldiers. Brigantia is a blend of wild Celtic spirit that has been punctuated with spears of Roman influence. She is untamed and wild but on the other side of the coin, she is reserved, calm and collected. Perhaps these two sides make her a contradiction. However different these faces of her appear, they are both embedded in her personality. These two extreme sides can also be found in diluted forms or in exaggerated forms in her other expressions of mother goddess, saint or dark mother in the appearances of Brigit, Brigid and Maman Brigitte.

Brigantia is a powerful archetype as queen and warrior that we can call upon in today's world. As a goddess of authority Brigantia can help us come face to face with our own power and bring that power out into the world through conscious and deliberate action. With her sword and battle shield, she will loan us her armour so that we too, can rise up in indignation and create healthy boundaries so that we aren't attacked again and again or that we don't keep ourselves small. As Queen of her tribe, Brigantia will inspire us to see our own crown, straighten it and move out of victimhood into empowerment. She will help us heed our inner call to inspired action that has the power to alter lives, our own first, then those of our tribe.

My initial attraction to Brigantia was driven by the curiosity to find out if she was a Roman deity or a Celtic deity or if she would reveal herself once more to be a blend that is most typical of how I know Brigid. I also really wanted to know if Brigantia is the predecessor of Brigid. I was intrigued by her war-like personality, how it differed from Brigid of Ireland, and I wondered how Pagan and Roman culture and society brought her into being. I did not perceive Brigantia as a gentle energy. Nor did I feel her as a dark goddess like Maman Brigitte. I sensed her as a mother goddess figure introduced to Britain from Gaul that became associated with war, by the Romans and then later by the Britons as a territorial guardian.

By penning this book, I am hoping to showcase this powerful side of Brigid known as Brigantia that we can call upon to guide us to our individual places of power. I am hoping that through her guidance we can get to a place within ourselves where we can stand strong and use our power to improve our own lives first and foremost, that of our communities, countries, nation, the world and the earth. I am hoping that through our connection with Brigantia that she will inspire sacred, channelled indignation and rage to mark our boundaries concerning senseless violence, law and order break down, gender violence, abuse in all forms and protection of the planet, her sacred body. Holy rage, sacred anger and positive aggression when we roar 'no', is what keeps us safe and reminds us of our strength. These are all crucial aspects of the divine feminine. This has the power to lift the shackles of fear in speaking our truth or doing our own thing for fear that it might cause war in our relationships and home life. Yet, drawing a circle of protection around our own worth can cause a positive ripple effect out into the world. The feminine has for too long been dissociated from indignation, rage and anger. Yet she has always been in these powerful emotions and states and always will be. Acting with love on behalf of what enrages us or breaks our hearts is what pushes us to become agents of change. This is not the same as inciting war.

We need a face of the goddess, in this case, a face of Brigid that can help those of us looking at war from afar and for those directly living through war. I want to share her aspects, which will give myself and you the reader, a way of noticing her, understanding her, appreciating her and a reason to connect with her when we are at war with ourselves, at war with our loved ones or at war with the atrocities happening in the world today.

As always when I journey with Brigid, I expect my inner world to reflect meeting and connecting to that powerful side of her. Brigantia took me on a deep journey to meet my relationship with my personal power. This involved me healing and bringing into balance my male energy. This was facilitated by the healer Miriam Shekinah who works with the goddess Cerridwen. On an outer level I travelled to a sacred territory of Brigantia to feel and connect to her very essence. Considering her as Earth goddess and lady of the land this was an obvious undertaking for me. My voyage led me to Northumberland, to Hadrian's Wall. I will talk about this in Chapter 4.

I now want to bring you the reader on a journey to meet Brigantia. I want to share my research with you and set the societal scene as it were before we look at archaeological evidence that has enabled me to weave together an image and discover a wonderful face of Brigid called Brigantia.

We will begin, in Chapter 1 in Pre-Roman and Roman Britain. We will look at Celtic life prior to the arrival of the Romans and consider how the Gauls influenced Celtic spirituality. In Chapter 2 we will consider Celtic society and how such warring tribes with such a reverence for war may have shaped Brigantia into being. Within Celtic society we will look at the warring role of women, and in particular, Boudicca of the Iceni tribe. In Chapter 3 we will focus on archaeological findings of Brigantia from the Roman Inscriptions of Britain. These provide us with imagery and dedications that help define the personality of Brigantia. Together we will take into consideration the Brigantian tribe and how they may have brought Brigantia to Ireland. We will also ponder the influence of the Roman Jupiter and Minerva and the African goddess Caelestis of Carthage on the personality of Brigantia. In Chapter 4 I recount my trip to Northumberland and also how I connect to Brigantia through animals, colours and symbols that I personally associate with her. These are influenced by the Roman inscriptions, but they are also my personal associations. In Chapter 5 I provide an overview of all that Brigantia stands for from my own point of view. I do hope that by the end of the book you, the reader, will be as enamoured by this unique aspect of Brigid's personality, as I am. I hope that my research will give you food for thought regarding her possible origins and what Brigantia could represent for us today. I hope that when it is time for you to be pushed into leading the life you were born to live, you will remember the queen archetype of Brigid that is waiting to assist you. I also hope that when you are on your own battlefield dealing with difficult times or trying to comprehend the atrocities of war in the world that she is someone you can connect to for comfort and for inspiration on how best to take action for your own betterment and for the betterment of those around you

A Note on Names

Throughout the book Brigid's name will appear in three different forms. As Celtic goddess she is Brigit, as Saint she is Brigid and as a Vodou deity she is Maman Brigitte or simply Brigitte. I typically spell the goddess and Saint collectively as Brigid but for the sake of clarity I will alternate the spelling of her name to highlight her various guises.

Chapter 1

Pre-Roman and Roman Britain

British Celts

The ancient Britons left no written record. As a result, our understanding of Britain in the Iron Age is incomplete. All information that we have about the Celts in general come from archaeological remains, medieval texts from Celtic languages and comments provided from Greek and Roman classical sources (Hutton, 2013). When reading the words from a colonizing pen we need to understand the that the written words were never without bias or an agenda. They were often written with political aims in mind (Macmillan, 2007) and either omitted important details or exaggerated unimportant issues (Aldhouse-Green, 2017). The Celts arrived in Britain and Ireland as early as 700 BC. They came trading, fleeing from war or just settling with others. As they moved and mingled throughout Europe, they imparted their habits and absorbed more of the same which resulted in areas of specific clusters of Celtic customs that still exist today, most notably in Ireland and Scotland, where Celtic languages are still spoken. As no written form existed during the time of the Celts and much of what we have today is a patchwork of findings, the collage of the various tribes of the Celts that has emerged is one that depicts a large but divided group of people that shared common traits, habits and spiritual beliefs.

Through the afore mentioned sources of archaeological remains, texts and comments we can get an image of who the ancient Britons were. This is important if we are to consider the backdrop against which Brigantia emerged. The British Celts were a diverse people, particularly according to region, culturally, genetically, and in terms of ethnic identity (Macmillan, 2007). In the Stone Age, people of Britain grew crops, kept animals and built settlements. The Bronze Age brought improvement in the form of tools, weapons and jewellery. In the late Bronze Age, the population grew, and people began to fight over land. People began to travel to Britain to trade in bronze and the country became known as far away as Greece and Rome. During the Bronze and Iron Ages until Rome invasion, waves of Celtic people moved across Europe in great migrations. Some settled in Britain as it was attractive for its tin and copper that could be used to make bronze. Despite great migrations across the continent of Europe, Hutton (2013) states that only 'minor intrusions' in the form of the Beaker people in the second millennium, and the Belgae in the later Iron Age came to Britain. The two types of Celts that came to Britain were the Goidels and the Belgae. The Goidels introduced the Bronze Age and the Belgae arrived later in the Iron Age (Hutton, 2013). Given their ancestry, if the goddess was not a feature of British Celtic spirituality, we can see how she may have arrived through these two groups. The Neolithic Age officially came to an end with the arrival of the Celts and the Bronze age began (Hutton, 2013). It was during the bronze Age that much trade took place and put Britain on the map as an attractive source of tin, from an imperial point of view.

Celts are generally classified as a group of people sharing common language, art and culture. What is generally most common amongst the Celtic world is the commonality of a Celtic language which may have been what was spread the most during the trading times of the Bronze Age. The spread of a language, may have carried with it some common cultural traits and values brought by traders, performers and artisans from the Atlantic seaboard eastward through Europe in the Bronze Age (Koch & Cunliffe, 2012).

The ancient Britons were not themselves one people, and the cultural and ethnic diversity among them was likely to be considerable (Macmillan (2007). Amongst the many tribes of the Celts there appears to be some degree of mutual belief or way of looking at the divine. What was common across Celtic religious practices and beliefs were the role of the Druids, horned deities, mother-goddesses, triplism, animism, shapeshifting and much more (Green, 2011). Macmillan (2007) describes the ancient Britons as a people who shared many cultural similarities with the Gauls resulting from trade and the exchange of goods. We will look at the specific influence of the Gauls on British Celtic life in Chapter 2.

Genetically the Britons shared similarities with the Basques of northern Spain and Southwest France. The Basques were presumed to be remnants of the 'Old European' (Gimbutas, 1999) which would mean the majority of the ancient British population were of similar origin. They were in fact as MacCulloch (2014) says, short dark people, called Iberians who were unlike the tall, fair skinned Belgae.

The religion of British Celts would undoubtedly have reflected such diversity and would contain within it, remnants of the Old European religion. It seems likely that their religion was the result of a Celtic culture then dominant in Europe combined with aspects of a more ancient indigenous belief system. What is most important for the context of this book about Brigantia is whether there existed goddess worship within British Celticism or whether the cult of the Goddess took off during Roman rule. It seems, that the goddess indeed was a feature of Celtic spirituality.

> It appears that in very ancient times the goddess was predominant in Britain and Ireland as she was in other very early (i.e. pre-Neolithic) Old European societies, and was parthogenic, or able to procreate without the help of a male god (Macmillan, 2007).

This is suggestive of her as a Mother Goddess figure. Her existence in Britain may have been as a result of Old European ancestral legacy brought in initially through the Belgae and the Goidels.

According to Gimbutas (1974) 'Old Europe' is applied to a pre-Indo-European culture of Europe, a culture which was matrifocal and probably matrilinear, agricultural and sedentary, egalitarian and peaceful. The religion of Old Europe, the era between 7000 and 3000 BC, focused on the wheel of life and its cyclical turning. According to Gimbutas (2001) the people of Old Europe worshipped goddesses, or a goddess, in many forms. Throughout the Neolithic period goddesses controlled birth giving, life sustenance, death bringing, and regeneration. The old European goddesses carried out these functions powerfully, as reflected by their physically strong portrayals in figurine and sculptural art. By classical times, the old European goddesses were eroticized, militarized to various degrees (especially Athena) and made subservient to the gods (Gimbutas, 2001).

Our journey back to the beginning of time to identify a single goddess deity is somewhat difficult. Virtually nothing is known about deities from the Neolithic area in Britain as nothing was recorded (Hutton, 2013). For British archaeologists, it was the held belief, mostly from the 1970's, that in the century beforehand, people venerated a goddess figure (Hutton, 2013). She appeared mostly in poetic works as an aspect of the romantic movement and as an antidote to excess civilization, urbanisation and industrialization that swept Europe in the decades around 1800 (Hutton, 2013). Evidence of a goddess-centered religion in the neolithic era is evidenced through archaeological finds in Turkey, Greece, the Balkans, the Aegean islands, Cyprus, Crete, Malta, Spain, Portugal and France (Gimbutas, 1974, 1991, 2001) but none have been found in Britain to denote a similar practice. (a Grimes Grave figurine was found but declared fake and another item in Somerset was considered a toy or a ritual object (Hutton, 2013).

Hutton (2013) argues against the notion of a single mother goddess concept of the Celtic world but suggests that the Celtic-speaking ancient Britons worshipped many goddesses. Macmillan (2007) is of the belief that there exists a single mother goddess figure:

> It appears that the Celtic-speaking ancient Britons worshipped many goddesses. It is, however, not clear if these were entirely separate deities, or if they were viewed as different aspects of the Great Mother herself (Macmillan, 2007).

Birnbaum (2001) brings us even further back in time, to over 100,000 years ago where she cites Africa as the original home of homo sapiens as well as the origins of the Dark African Mother who went with African migrants as they walked and sailed to every corner of the world (Birnbaum, 2001). Such viewpoints for and against the existence of the Great Mother Goddess in Celtic Britain is pertinent to how we consider Brigantia. As there is no definitive answer, we remain unsure and can only speculate.

Old European religion that held the goddess sacred, influenced not only British and Irish spiritual practices but also those of the Etruscans, Greeks and the Romans (Gimbutas, 2001). For me this is where the waters start to muddy and the blending or fusing of cultures and practices begin. The Romans, as we will later see, did not have a uniform religious practice themselves. They had absorbed African, Near Eastern, Greek and Etruscan cults into their own religion and would bring these influences to new lands that they conquered.

During the ensuing proto-Indo-European culture the female deities, or more accurately the Goddess Creatrix in her many aspects, were largely replaced by the predominantly male divinities of the Indo-Europeans, to whom belonged the Romans. (Gimbutas, 1974). What developed after c. 2500 BC was a mélange of the two mythic systems, Old European and Indo-European (Gimbutas, 1974).

It is within this mélange of Old European and Indo-European, that I focus my attention, on a most unique deity to emerge from these worlds known as Brigantia. From the Dark African Mother to the Old European matrifocal pantheon and British Celticity, we meet a mother goddess deity, who during the period of migration and invasion was viewed by her people as sovereign protector of the land. She also underwent a transmutation as society changed. During this transformation, the Old European mother goddess who was warm and protective showed another side to her. A side that showed she was ready to take up arms and fight, that she was someone to be feared. This is evidenced from writings on Roman Inscriptions in Britain which we will look at in more detail in Chapter 3. Her transformation was also physical. Her name and veneration spread from the northern hilltops of Northumberland across the lands and possibly across the sea into Ireland. With the expansion of her name and veneration, I feel her image and status also evolved from mother to queen. Perhaps she needed a new identity to face the greatest conquerors of all time, the Romans, or indeed her gaining prominence and power was deliberate by the Romans to reflect the effect Imperialists were having and could have on ordinary civilians if they would simply succumb to Roman rule.

Roman Invasion

The first Roman invasion of Britain was in 55 BC led by Julius Caesar. This was a failure for the common observer looking on but as far as Caesar was concerned, he had captured the Roman public imagination, that he, Caesar, could go anywhere and do anything (Russell & Laycock, 2011). The Romans were defeated but returned in 54 BC with Caesar once again as overseer. For nearly one hundred years Britain was left alone before the third and final invasion, led by Emperor Claudius proved to be successful. They subjugated the south first before gaining control of the whole island. The northern tribes were the most resistant and were described as the savage tribes at the other side of Hadrian's Wall (Strong, 2018). One of the tribes to the north were called the Brigantes and took their name from our goddess in question; Brigantia. The first exposed piece of her personality possibly lies within this fact. The imperialists changed the name of their new lands from Albion to Britannia. What made Britain so attractive to one of the most powerful forces at that time? Njai (2013) tells us that they came to Britain to plunder and take home wealth, but also because it served as a place of refuge for dissident Gauls (Njai, 2013).

The Gauls, as mentioned earlier, were a Celtic people who lived in an agricultural society divided into several tribes ruled by a landed class. They had settled in a region named Gaul by the Romans that comprises modern-day France, parts of Belgium, Switzerland, Luxembourg, the Netherlands, western Germany and northern Italy. Caesar's Gallic war (58-50 BC) is seen as a deliberate act of genocide, a Celtic holocaust during which two-thirds of an estimated population of three million either perished or were enslaved and which paved the way for five centuries of Roman rule. Roman wars were fought in Gaul, led by Caesar in an effort to expand the territory of the republic. The Britons had supported the Gauls in their attempts to resist Roman forces. During the Roman invasions, some Gauls had escaped to Britain as fugitives (Ellis Beresford, 2013).

By the end of the first century the Romans controlled most of southern Britain, including Wales and gradually Scotland. Unlike in Gaul there was no such widespread disruption and loss of life in Britain, whose tribal networks seem to have remained largely in place and in some areas positively encouraged and nurtured (Russell & Laycock, 2011). Roads, comfortable homes, town baths and town walls were introduced by the Romans. New ways of living such as living in towns, visiting public baths, watching plays and chariot races and speaking Latin were adopted into Celtic culture. Along with new ways of living and doing things came sophistication, domesticity, entertainment, rich food and civilisation. Some welcomed the good life and embraced what was on offer. Those pro Roman started to copy Roman dress and traditions to gain better position or status. As recompense, Roman credit markets opened to the Britons if they joined. They used this to buy luxuries, only dreamed of before (Njai, 2013). Many Britons became more Roman than Celtic at this time, but that wasn't the case for all. Many vehemently opposed the new occupiers and hid in the forests and swamps refusing to submit. In addition to the Brigantes of the north, Celts in Wales, and Cornwall held tight to keep their customs. They came out of hiding sometimes and attacked small Roman forts or outposts. But there was no grand overthrow. Britain remained part of the Roman Empire for almost four hundred years (Strong, 2018). In the early 5th Century, Rome itself was under almost constant attack from tribes outside the Empire. More troops were needed to defend Rome and other parts of the Empire, so the Roman army was eventually withdrawn from Britain. The Anglo-Saxons arrived to replace Roman occupation. The new English conquered nearly all of England, save Wales, Scotland and Cornwall.

The consequences of the Roman presence in Britain were several. For the first time Britons were introduced to taxation and the mining of tin as well as some agricultural practices were abolished. The most fundamental change in British Celtic life under Roman rule was the abolishment of the power of the Druids. Druids were the intellectual class of the Celts and were at the centre of Celtic society. They were priests, philosophers, judges, educators, historians, doctors, seers, astronomers and astrologers (Ellis, 1994). Up until Roman occupation they had the final say on all matters both private and public. They made decisions on matters of tradition, customs and law and also on general questions concerning nature and human life (Ó hÓgáin, 2006). The Druids were eradicated by the Romans for their practice of human sacrifice, (Strong, 2018).

'Roman culture was itself a cosmopolitan fusion of influences with very diverse points of origin' (Hutton, 2013). These 'diverse points of origin' reflect the Old European religion but mostly classical Greece. Strong similarities exist between Greek and Roman mythologies possibly coming from the two cultures' similar experience of the Southern European region and the Mediterranean Sea. After the Romans came into contact with the Greek culture, some Roman divinities began to reflect the qualities of Greek gods and goddesses (Akgoz, 2020). Roman civilisation had spread across western Europe, North Africa and eastern Asia throughout the sixth to first centuries BC. As Rome took control of these areas, making parts of Europe, Africa and Asia 'Roman', so Rome the city itself became more European, African and Asian (Russell & Laycock, 2011).

The Romans were highly literate. They wrote down their myths in the Latin language relatively early in Roman history, even though the originals may have been told in the Greek world hundreds of years earlier. Roman mythologies tried to explain the founding and history of their nation. It is little wonder that their divinities were brought with them as they continued to plunder lands in an attempt to expand their power.

Roman deities were divine and semi divine beings. They tended to be functional and had uniquely distinctive attributes which meant that a particular request, prayer or dedication could be directed to a specific deity (Russell & Hutton, 2011). They presided over cereal farming, agriculture, manure, childbirth and war. (Hutton, 2013). Strictly speaking, there was no native Roman mythology about divine beings – no home-grown traditions of their origins, deeds and family relationships, although Greek myths about equivalent deities became attached to those of Rome as part of the general Roman acquisition of many traits of Greek culture (Hutton, 2013). The Greeks themselves had acquired this from the Near East.

The Romans were open to new cults arriving from foreign lands. Perhaps the most assimilated deity of all into Roman culture was Isis. The worship of Isis reached Rome early in the first century BC. Isis was the Egyptian goddess of love, fertility, resurrection and magic. The priests and priestesses who served her were known for their healing powers associated with magic. Her cult was a mystery religion that required initiation. This is possibly where the role of priestesses originated. By the early first century her cult was flourishing throughout Europe. Isis was part of a triad with Serapis and Harpocrates their son. Triplism exists notably with Brigid. Isis was a goddess of fertility and marriage. She was depicted as loving and compassionate, especially as a loving mother, often like the image we see of the Virgin Mary and Christ. Isis was also portrayed with a ritual bucket for holy Nile water and a rattle. Maybe this is where we learned in the west of the sanctity of the water, as the waters of the goddess. Both water and the rattle were used in her worship. Her headdress was a sun disc surrounded by a crescent moon or cow's horn (Adkins & Adkins, 1996). This symbolism is too big to ignore in connection to Brigid. As both goddess and saint Brigid features in myths of beams of light and fire coming from her head as well as having the cow as perhaps her most sacred animal. Three of Brigid's most common symbols, the vulture, serpent and the cow were all symbols of the goddess Isis (Condren, 1989).

It's safe to say that the Romans were quite open-minded about assimilating other cultures into their own and, likewise, Romans travelling abroad would take with them the rites dedicated to their familiar divine beings and expect, very often, to honour the deities of the lands which they entered

(Hutton, 2013). Rome was quite happy to tolerate mostly all belief systems that it encountered during its campaign of conquest. The absorption of local non-Roman cults, gods and goddesses into the imperial system was conducted primarily because of the deeply superstitious nature of the Roman mind, in which it was felt important to get the indigenous spirits of conquered peoples on the side of the new government (Russell & Laycock, 2011). It may also have been a well thought out strategy to win over the locals and appear to be on their side. To the British there would have been nothing very alien about the essence of the religious system that the Roman conquerors brought with them (Hutton, 2013). This may be because worship of the goddess, albeit in a maternal fertility-based cult was already in operation, possibly, as mentioned earlier, having been brought to Britain by the Goidels, Belgae and the Gauls. British Celts may themselves have had a similar laxness as it were of local gods and goddesses and so could identify with the Roman loose pantheon of gods and goddesses that were borrowed and assimilated into their own culture. It could also be that the gods of war most important to the Romans had an appealing lure to the Britons who were often described as barbaric or savage and quick to combat (Russell & Laycock, 2011).

Roman religion was practical rather than an individual practice which solidifies even more the male-like warring characteristics of their goddesses. Each god or goddess had a clearly defined role and uniquely distinctive attributes which meant that a particular request, prayer or dedication could be directed to a particular deity (Russell & Laycock, 2011). The warlike association with their goddess may simply be a reflection of what was pertinent to the Roman; invasion, conquering and expansion. Or maybe their female deities were hardened up from the more nurturing Earth mother type and a deliberate act of instigating a more patriarchal approach to life and governance. Roman goddesses, like their Greek counterparts were goddesses of wisdom, love, war and the sky. These traits, in varying degrees would also feature in Brigantia and later Brigid, who, I argue, can be considered a possible progeny of Brigantia.

As mentioned earlier, it is worth noting that Roman religion and culture was heavily influenced by the Etruscans. The Etruscans were an ancient Italic people who inhabited modern-day Tuscany, known in Roman times as Etruria. They pre-dated the Romans as earliest civilizers on the Italian peninsula. They were eventually driven out by the Romans long after their culture was assimilated into that of the Romans. Etruscan influence on Roman culture included making images of deities and forming divine triads. Romans took their alphabet for writing Latin, they took their temple plans, the art of divination and even the famous Roman toga dress came from the Etruscans. What's noteworthy is that Etruscan women were liberated to a degree that was not common amongst their Greek and Roman counterparts. Etruscan women were free. They exercised unashamedly in the nude with men and other women. They practised matrifocal customs until their customs were blended into obsoletion into Roman customs. This meant they raised their own children and gave them her name and she was free to own her own property. Etruscan women liked to drink and dressed in a manner similar to that of men. They even wore symbols of citizenship and rank. Their names reflected their legal and social status. Conversely, Roman women were either the property of their fathers or their husbands carrying one name or the others. Etruscan women played important roles as priestesses and seers and were a force in politics. Etruscan women were literate and were often buried in elaborate tombs.

Initial Roman gods included Jupiter, the supreme god, Mars, the god of war and father of Romulus and Remus, and Quirinus, the deified Romulus who watched over the people of Rome. This triad later became the trinity of Jupiter, the supreme god,

Juno, his wife/sister who was identified with the Greek goddess Hera, and Minerva, Jupiter's daughter (Akgoz, 2020). Minerva was identified with Athena, the Greek goddess of wisdom and war. Already we saw triplism with Isis, Brigid of Ireland and now once more with Jupiter, Juno and Minerva. The inclusion of women into this trio is important and the traits associated with them. If we can understand the characteristics and significance of these Roman gods and goddesses, then we can understand the attributes of the British deities, such as Brigantia, that peered out from behind the Roman masks. We will look at the personalities of relevant Roman gods and goddesses linked to Brigantia in Chapter 3.

Of all the gods that came with the Romans, Mars was readily adopted by the Celts. The Italian Mars originally had an agricultural role in Italy as guardian of the fields and possibly too as a storm-god (Green, 2011). If this aspect of Jupiter was showcased by the Romans, we can understand how easily Jupiter would have been accepted by a people so closely attuned to dependency upon the land. We can also possibly view the agricultural connection of Jupiter to the earth mother in both the personalities of Brigantia and Brigid. But in his truest essence, Mars was a war god and as such he represented what was most dear to the Romans. When the Romans arrived in Britain, they were met with a highly combative population that were no strangers to fighting. Fighting was done by both men and women which was not the case in Roman culture. This might possibly be a reason why Brigantia rose in prominence with Roman presence in Britain; a goddess of the land for all her people, a goddess for practical matters in defending their territory, as observed in the Roman cult, but also a goddess for combative women, defending their land alongside men.

The question at this point is whether Brigantia was an honoured deity in Britain before the arrival of the Romans or whether she was completely fabricated by the Romans. If we had a definitive answer as to whether the Mother Goddess was venerated in Celtic Britain, our answer would be more obvious but it is not. Given the Roman custom of honouring native deities of the British and encouraging the natives themselves to do so (Hutton, 2013) we are therefore, unclear about whether Brigantia was venerated in Britain before imperial rule. Salway (1965) posits that she is Roman fabrication; stating that 'All the evidence points to the purely Roman creation of a cantonal deity and none to a survival from Celtic religion' (Salway, 1965). Joliffe (1941) concurs and adds that:

> ...she must be considered within a Roman framework rather than Celtic myth especially as her cult belongs to the reign of Severus and Caracalla and must be interpreted against the background of the ideas and history of that period. (Jolliffe, 1941).

Hutton (2013, however, claims she may indeed have been its main deity before the Romans arrived. 'Brigantia's warring qualities have undoubtedly been influenced by her Roman side. These qualities also come from her Celtic side' (Hutton, 2013).

Chapter 2

War, Death and the Celts

The Celts and War

The Celtic world covered most of Western and Central Europe and with colonies as far as Asia Minor. The heart of the Celtic world was in the area between the Rhineland and the upper Danube basin (Hutton, 2013). We can perchance acknowledge the existence of a single, great mother goddess from this as the river Danube was named after the Celtic mother Danu (Ellis, 1994). Danu is called an early mother of unyielding fertility (Ellis, 1994) but she is also the death goddess, the neolithic vulture goddess and tomb goddess (Gimbutas, 2001). Her dualistic nature is significant as war and death were inextricably linked and interconnected in Celtic society. (Green, 2011) quotes Caesar who remarked that:

> The Druids attach particular importance to the belief that the soul does not perish but passes after death from one body to another; they think that this belief is the most effective way to encourage bravery, because it removes the fear of death. (Green, 2011).

The Celts were first and foremost warriors. They lived in groups of tribal societies with fixed boundaries that were heavily protected. They were ferocious in battle and always ready to defend and attack. Each tribe consisted of several families and had its own king or chieftain whose main preoccupation was to act in connection to warfare or to make decisions regarding relationships with other tribes. Societal ranking included the druids at the top followed by the kings, followed by the noble, the free but not noble and the unfree (Ellis, 1994). The Celts were always on their guard and prepared for attack.

War-princes ride to battle in chariots, collect enemy heads as trophies, display feats of skill and valour and indulge both in constant local battles and in individual fighting between champions (Green, 2011).

These combative people were part of a warrior-elite society. Warriors were sons and daughters of nobility and were second in ranking only to the tribal king. Warriors were buried with their weaponry in rich and elaborate graves. Their graves not only suggest the wealth of this warrior-elite class but also a belief in the afterlife where material items such as weaponry were needed, and their prestigious earthly status was retained. The Celts were skilled miners and brilliant metal workers. They made all kinds of weapons and tools to clear new land, plough fields, build homes and then defend them. They also made weaponry and helmets for combat. The Celts were skilled at rearing horses, which they used for war, hunting, farming and transport.

The Celts were described by the Romans as barbarians or savage, possibly due to the head-taking custom in battle. They had a natural predisposition to conflict which spilled out into their everyday living. Chance remarks at feasting times could easily escalate in fighting. Also, during feasts, it was customary for the most heroic in battle to take the thigh piece of meat. If someone disputed this they stood up and fought in single combat to death (Ellis, 1995). Ellis (1995) cites Strabo who also remarks on the easily awakened fighting spirit of the Celt. 'They assemble in large numbers on slight provocation, being ever ready to sympathise with the anger of a neighbour who thinks he has been wronged' (Ellis, 1995). They often engaged in mock battles to be ready, just in case. War symbolised the life-death-rebirth and the struggle of light, life and prosperity against opposing negative forces.

Many are said to have gone into battle naked. In doing so, they believed they would release their karma to full potential and enhance their powers and that, if killed, they would quickly incarnate in the Otherworld (Ellis, 1994). Njai (2013) quotes Churchill, who reports that Caesar said of the Celts:

> All the Britain's indeed dye themselves with woad, which occasions a blueish color, and thereby has a more terrible appearance in fight (Njai, 2013).

Green (2011) mentions a special group of riders who brandish 'sword or spear in a gesture of ecstasy is usually naked and female' (Green, 2011).

Mock battles were custom as part of military drill. Things could sometimes get out of hand and in such cases if bystanders didn't intervene death could result. The Celts considered it a glory to die and a disgrace to survive without victory. The bodies of the dead were often left to the crows to devour. 'The war-goddess, or perhaps more accurately the mother-goddess in her war mien, was believed by them to appear in the form of such a bird' (O hÓgáin, 2022). Most interesting is the name given to skill development in becoming a warrior. Brigandage was the custom of joining a tribe or gang to develop and survive on the skills of raiding other tribes. As this was done outside the locality, it was not considered an offense nor an embarrassment. (O hÓgáin, 2002). I can't help but see the name of this warrior custom as a link to Brigantia.

The Influence of Gaul

Celtic groups had been settling in Britain since the early 6th century or thereabouts (O hÓgáin, 2002). The earliest of groups were those displaced in Gaul. Gaul was a region of

Western Europe, encompassing present-day France, Belgium, Luxembourg, parts of Switzerland, Netherlands, Germany and Northern Italy. Gaul was divided into three parts: Gallia Celtica, Belgica and Aquitanian. Gauls arrived in Britain at the end of the 3rd century and brought their martial ways with them (Ó hÓgáin, 2002). When Belgic tribes spread into northern Gaul significant sections of these began to cross into Britain. The Belgae took over most of the Southern British coast and large stretches of territory inland. In time they established strong kingdoms. These were accomplished seafarers and traders as well as adept in military skills. They were developing coinage and very significantly, they brought the Mother-Goddess with them. Caesar is said to have noted similarities between Britain and Gaul (Green, 2012).

> The Mother-Goddess cult, so dominant in Gaul and Britain during the Romano-Celtic period, must have its origin during Celtic pre-history, simply because of its occurrence almost entirely in Celtic territory (Green, 2011).

They also may have brought the warring personality of the great mother with them that would later influence the character of Brigantia:

> The divine Mother is represented with the symbols of life and abundance, but her images were buried in tombs with the dead, and moreover, she has a destructive element in having very direct associations with warfare (Green, 2011).

Celtic Women and War

What makes Celtic and Gaulish society interesting is the role women within these societies played. If Brigantia can be considered a warrior goddess, her dual aspects of mother and warrior would undoubtedly have been venerated. Comprising of both maternal and military, she was most likely a role model for women. Gaulish women were notoriously strong and brave:

> A whole troop of foreigners would not be able to withstand a single Gaul if he called his wife to his assistance, who is usually very strong and with blue eyes; especially when, swelling her neck, gnashing her teeth, and brandishing her sallow arms of enormous size, she begins to strike blows mingled with kicks, as if they were so many missiles sent from the string of a catapult. (Njai, 2013).

Celtic women were great in stature, strong and blue-eyed and courageous like their male counterparts. They could choose their husbands, own property and fight in wars. Women served as priestesses, prophetesses, chieftainesses. They took and held prisoners of war. They acted as negotiators. Women could inherit property and retain all rights to the property even in marriage. Women were free to choose their own husbands or lovers and had equal rights to divorce (Ellis, 2013). Females were seen as direct descendants from the Mother Goddess. They were respected as leaders, most notably, in protecting their territory.

Green (2011) references writers who speak of the valour, indomitably and sheer physical strength of Gaulish women who were just as formidable in war as their husbands. She proposes that Celtic women had a more passive role in warfare but an important role, nonetheless. In Europe the role of women was supportive. Their presence encouraged their men to fight with might and their visual presence protected them from abduction, rape and capture. Standing on the battlefield with men was also a spiritual statement as the whole community came together and invoked divine assistance in battle. In Britain women were placed on carts at the edge of the battlefield, where they could have a good view and join unison to their men with war cries, howls and insults. Present but out of harm's way they stood alongside men and screamed for victory (Green, 1997). Even if women had a predominantly passive role in war they were, like men, killed and wounded in battle. Just like men, they went down fighting.

Two major fighting females that had anything but a passive role in British history are Cartimandua and Boudicca. Out of the two, it is Boudicca, Queen of the Iceni tribe who is most renowned and respected for her valiant feats.

Boudicca

Anwyl (1906) quotes Dio who describes Boudicca thusly:

> She was huge of frame, terrifying of aspect, and with a harsh voice. A great mass of bright red hair fell to her knees. She wore a great twisted golden necklace, and a tunic of many colours, over which was a thick mantle fastened by a brooch. Now she grasped a spear, to strike fear into all who watched her. (Anwyl, 1906).

Boudicca ruled the Iceni tribe of East Anglia, that takes in Norfolk and parts of Suffolk and Cambridgeshire with her husband King Prasutagus. When he died, he left half of his possessions to the emperor hoping that his family would be protected. But the Romans confiscated his property, increased taxation, and drove nobles out of the estate (Njai, 2013). Boudicca protested. She was publicly flogged, and her daughters raped. Boudicca unified some of the British tribes and waged war. At the helm, she and her army destroyed three Roman towns of the former capital Colchester, London, and Saint Albans (Ó hÓgáin, 2002). It is said that she drove in her chariot around tribe after tribe, encouraging them and saying that she was there, not as a noble, 'but as one of the people, avenging my lost freedom, my scourged body, and the outraged chastity of my daughters' (Ó hÓgáin, 2002).

It was at Watling Street that her huge army was defeated by the waiting and more skilful Romans. Over 80,000 Britons were killed at the hands of the Romans in revenge. Rather than face capture, Boudicca took her own life through poison. Worse was to come. The Britons had expected to beat the Romans and had not sowed crops. A famine resulted. Rome eventually came to help, and Britain slowly settled down into Roman rule. Celto-Roman assimilation began. Classical roman deities started to amalgamate with Celtic deities.

Interestingly, Boudicca was a priestess of Andrasta, goddess of battle, sovereignty and victory which seems to be the same goddess as Andarta, worshipped by the Vocontii of Gaul (Beresford-Ellis, 2013). Andrasta was revered for her strength and power and invoked for a positive outcome in combat. Boudicca herself, although she killed thousands, is viewed as a strong woman who fought for her freedom and justice. Queens Elizabeth I and Victoria are compared to Boudicca. Elizabeth I is said to have claimed that she descended from the same family as Boudica. Elizabeth I had the same colour hair and spoke to her army just like Boudicca before battle. Queen Victoria's husband Albert commissioned a statue of Boudicca and her daughters riding a war chariot to celebrate her long reign. Boudicca vibes abound when it comes to women's issues of equality. In the mid-19th century women carried fabric banners through the streets of London bearing Boudicca's name and her picture appeared on posters as they campaigned for the right to vote. Boudicca stood for rising up, taking charge and defending her and her tribes' rights, whether that tribe was local, national or a tribe of women. She has also been portrayed as a loving and protective mother by the sculptor J Harvard Thomas through his statue of Boudicca and her daughters in Cardiff city hall.

Boudicca, for me, embodied Brigantia's warrior energy. As fierce warrioress she gave it her all and stood tall, spear in hand, screaming, no. No to invasion of her country, no to injustice and no to violence against women. Bridging the gap and unifying the divided tribes of Britain she took the lead against Roman invasion and how she and her daughters were treated. As she rode out, her following and army grew by bringing other tribes on board. Before the battle she asked her goddess for a sign. A hare was released, and it ran to the right symbolising a fortuitous outcome. Described by Bulst (1961) as more than a queen by her ability to produce a remarkable omen before battle and invoke the goddess, the ultimate Warrior Queen of the Iceni instigated the revolt, led the revolt, inspired and motivated tribes and flattened Roman presence as she trailblazed her way through Colchester, London and St Albans. As news of her attack in London spread to Wales, Roman plans to subdue Celts in northern Wales who had fled England had to be put on hold. Although she did not win the battle, she stood up and took action against injustice.

Celtic Deities

Unlike Roman state religion, there does not seem to have been a universal family of gods and goddesses within Iron Age Britain and north-western Europe. Rather, deities, may have been specific to particular tribes, clans or family groups. Spirits were, as far as it is possible to tell, probably associated with natural features in the landscape, such as a spring, river, mountain, hill or forest (Russell & Laycock, 2011).

Within the complex tapestry of the Celtic world was a common, golden thread that was woven into the fabric of Celtic spirituality. The Celtic world shared the worship of a high exalted goddess that contained the root -bri in her many various name forms. I will consider these in more detail in Chapter 3.

Celtic goddesses primarily held a territorial role (Green, 2011), as well as being local or tribal in character (Anwyl, 1906). The emergence of local and territorial deities arises out of societal development and needs. The need was per chance defence and protection and a harder side of the mother goddess on whom they could lean. As Leeming and Fee (2016) says 'the faces of God and Goddess always reflect the souls of the people who worship them'. The Celts had an emphasis on territory, most notably expanding and protecting it. In comparison to the Romans or Greeks, Celtic society was basic. It was also mongrel, heavily influenced by Europe and the middle East. This would surely feature in their deities, like Brigantia. Anwyl (1906) states there was undoubtedly a goddess of Britain. And 'of British goddesses, Brigantia is one of the most important' (Anwyl, 1906). He also attests 'It is not improbable that Brigantia was the tribal deity of the powerful tribe of the Brigantes of the north of England' (Anwyl, 1906). This leads us nicely to the most important part of the book. It is time now to meet our goddess in focus, Brigantia.

Chapter 3

Brigantia

Brigantia

Brigantia, the name of the 'High one' that comes from the tribal designation of the Brigantes (Jolliffe, 1941). The goddess Brigantia is found on three Romano-British inscriptions and four others which contain the abbreviated forms -Brig, Brigan and Brigant. They are assumed to all refer to the same goddess (Jolliffe, 1941). With the exception of Birrens, all inscriptions to Brigantia are on altars, which also signifies her as the 'High one'. This highness may reference the literal meaning of -Brig which is high, as in raised or high as in exalted, in a spiritual sense. The cognate 'Briga' must also have denoted force, vigour, nobility and sacredness, especially when referring to deities (Beck, 2009), and possibly also her intellect, divine origin or even her sovereign highness.

From Chapter 1 we considered whether Brigantia was originally a Celtic British deity, whether she came with the Romans, or if she was the result of a cultural syncretism between Rome and Britain. From a linguistic perspective, however, we can place her into a more obvious category than the other. Brigantia's name is undoubtedly Celtic (Beck, 2009). It comes from the Gaulish word -briga. It is a cognate with old Irish -brí, Cornish, Welsh and Bretin -bre, hill, denoting a high place that is a hill or a mount (Beck, 2009). Given then, that she may probably be a Celtic deity we can see evidence for this in river names that are connected to Brigantia. The river names Braint (Anglesey) and Brent (Middlesex) are derived from a form of Brigantia. Water was sacred to the Celts (Green, 2011). Water, for the Celts, that included wells, rivers and springs was often the setting for supernatural events. The importance of waters is confirmed based on votive deposits found in water bodies (Fairless, 1989). Wells such as those found at Vindolanda in Northumberland predate Roman occupation. Further linguistic evidence for Brigantia's Celtic origin are found in British place names such as Brentford (Middlesex), South Brent and Brentor (Devonshire) and East Brent (Somerset) (Jolliffe, 1941). However:

> The connection of these names with the Romano-British Brigantia is not obvious. Possibly the word was an honorific epithet for both rivers and hills of peculiar sanctity, which was associated in northern Britain with a more definitive divine personality (Jolliffe, 1941).

It should be noted that other place names in Europe also bear her name. Brigantia's name is found in Bregenz, Austria. In France, we find her name in Briançonnet and Briançon, found in Provence-Alpes-Côte d'Azur. In Hungary, she is in Brigetio. In Portugal the ancient name of Bragança in Trás-os-Montes, was Brigantia. and in Spain the cities of A Coruña and Betanzos in Galicia were named Brigantia and Brigantium.

If we take our linguistic evidence and consider her as a Celtic goddess and understand her trajectory from the Dark African mother that came with the Celts into Britain, we can understand her as a mother goddess figure. 'Above the gods were the 'mother of the gods' Anu/Danu/ Don or Brigit/ Brigantia' (Ross, 1970). As mother figure she may have evolved out of the northern territory and is as Beresford Ellis says 'a British Celtic motherland image to serve the English purpose in unifying the nations of the British Isles under English rule' (Beresford Ellis, 1995).

Within the mother goddess image, we can identify her as the tutelary goddess of the Brigantes tribe, who took their name from her (Jolliffe, 2014). Beck (2013) has shown that she is more than the personification of the Brigantes, but is a goddess in her own right. Her areas of concern included protecting the tribe, ensuring prosperity and fertility in the home and inspiring success in the learning arts, especially poetry (Nicholson, 1999). She is also the unifier, as mentioned above. The aforementioned characteristics are all depicted on the statue of Brigantia of Birrens in England, now kept in the National Museum of Scotland in Edinburgh, where she stands tall as a tower of strength. We will look at all the inscriptions dedicated to her in detail later in this chapter. What has been the source of fascination for me with Brigantia was MacCulloch's (2014) claim that Brigantia's popularity is seen 'in the *continuation* of her personality and cult in those of Saint Brigit' (MacCulloch, 2014). This really was what prompted me to research Brigantia to see if she was the proto of Brigid. I wanted to see if there were characteristics of Brigantia that were recognizable in Brigid. Within her evident features from the Birrens relief we can certainly see similarities between Brigantia and Brigid especially in those mentioned by Nicholson (1999), in her areas of prosperity, fertility in the home, success in the learning arts and poetry.

As unifier, Brigantia could be regarded as the symbol of the British Empire as Britannia. 'We have here undoubtedly a goddess of Britain' (Anwyl, 1906). In addition, Brigantia was also associated with healing (Ross, 1997). This is in keeping with her as mother goddess, her role as tribal protector and with her connection to water. On an inscription at Hadrian's Wall, she is referenced as a nymph. This connection to water and healing is once more indicative of Brigid of Ireland.

We are still undecided about her divine origins. She may be Celtic, but she may also be classical. For a start, if it wasn't for the Romans' custom of regularly making images of divine beings in stone and metal, and writing dedications to them in the same durable materials, we wouldn't have our information of her today (Hutton, 2013). That aside, it cannot be denied that under Roman rule, Brigantia not only flourished but gained prominence (Jolliffe, 1941).

Brigantia is sometimes equated with Victoria, the Roman goddess of victory. This is evidenced in the sculptured relief from Birrens, North of Hadrian's Wall, wearing wings and a mural crown. These are also typically associated with Victoria. She also carries a spear, shield and a gorgon Aegis which are symbols associated with Minerva, another Roman deity to whom she is compared. Undoubtedly, as we will see, there are strong classical overtones in her personality that are evidenced from Roman Inscriptions in Britain. What is difficult to know, is whether the conquerors laid a classical mediterranean veneer over the native system (Hutton, 2013) as an act of respect and reverence for local deities or indeed if Brigantia was deliberately imposed on a number of shrines all over northern Britain (only evidence for two though) in order to effect uniformity of cult as an aid to easy administration. (Jolliffe, 1941).

Roman Inscriptions of Britain

What we lack in epigraphic evidence for Brigantia from Celtic Britain, we have in a miniscule amount in the form of Roman Inscriptions of Britain. From blended figure images, and written dedications, we can get some sense as to who Brigantia was for her people. The various Roman inscriptions provide us with some evidence of a particular personality. Within these inscriptions we can see a nod to both the Celtic and Imperial world. One could argue that beneath the Roman surface lies an original Celtic Brigantia or one could argue that she rose to prominence through the Roman lens, because she was indeed, of Roman creation. Whatever conclusion you might come to, know that her essence, her personality, is truly one of a kind, a unique blend of wild cultures and powerful civilisations.

On Roman Inscriptions of Britain (R.I.B) we find seven inscriptions to her either solely as the goddess Brigantia or as a combined deity with Victoria, Jupiter, Caelistis, Salus. This continues the debate concerning her Celtic or Roman essence. To make it more interesting, on inscriptions she is sometimes called a nymph or is referenced in her masculine form as Bregnus. We will now look at each inscription and detect symbolism within both the written dedications and the images to uncover a precise personality unique to Brigantia.

RIB 630

RIB 630 was discovered on a Roman site at Adel. The dedicant it would seem is female. The inscription reads:

> Deae Brigantiae \ donum cinge \ tissa posuit
> *To the goddess Brigantia, Cingetissa set up this offering.*

The name Cingetissa means warrior or attacker (Becks, 2009). The inscription is engraved on a sandstone altar which has a serpent on its left side. If we acknowledge the image of the serpent which is synonymous with healing, we can consider Brigantia as a healing deity (Fairless, 1949). What is interesting about this inscription as well as the inscription at South Shields is that the dedicant is of Celtic stock. This shows the attachment of indigenous people to their roots and beliefs (Beck, 2009). It may also highlight the female as warrior and her connection to an archetype to support her in this role. This could be interpreted as symbolic of her warring Celtic heritage.

RIB 628

An altar at Castleford dedicated to Victoria Brigantia bears the following inscription:

Deae Vic\toriae Brigantiae\aram dedicavit Aurelius S\ enopianus
To the goddess Victoria Brigantia Aurelius Senopianus dedicated this altar.

RIB 2091

At Birrens the following is dedicated to Brigantia:

Brigantiae sacrum Amandus\architectus ex imperio imperatum fecit
Sacred to Brigantia: Amandus, the engineer, by command fulfilled the order.

The Birrens image provides sufficient detail about Brigantia that helps bring her identity to light. On this inscription she is dressed in a tunic and a cloak. On her breast is a small medallion of a gorgon's head. She holds a spear in her right hand and a globe in her left. On her head is a helmet bordered by a mural crown. She is also winged. To the right of the figure is an omphaloid or sacred stone. At a first glance we detect Minerva, which gives her an immediate Roman feel. The only Celtic symbolism is the 'barbaric coiffure and the helmet with horns attached' (Jolliffe, 1941). Because of the wings which are typically associated with Victory, she may be called Minerva Victrix. Portrayed with shield, spear, aegis and wings the warrior goddess appears strong and well able to defend her people and her land. 'I suggest tentatively that she was the divine guardian of the new colony of York and that from there the cult was to be carried to the rest of the province' (Jolliffe, 1941).

Because Minerva Victrix was a warrior goddess, we can potentially place Brigantia into the same category. In her portrayal as a Minerva figure, she once more is identifiable as a healing goddess. Healing was a function of the Gallic Minerva and is to be seen in Britain too, most notably in the case of the Romano-British goddess presiding over the waters of Bath, namely Sulis-Minerva (Fairless, 1941). It is possible that at Birrens, Brigantia superseded a local water-goddess who had already surrendered her identity to Minerva (Jolliffe, 1941).

In the relief at Birrens, Brigantia is depicted as territorial goddess. The goddess wears a mural crown indicating her function as city or regional goddess (Jolliffe, 1941 Named after the Brigantes, we can only assume that she embodied her tribe. In Graeco-Roman art, the crown is the mark of Tyche-Fortuna who was the protecting goddess of the city (Jolliffe, 1941). Her role is therefore an obvious one as sovereign protectress of her peoples. But the question is whether she was intended to be the goddess of the whole province? Her mural crown suggests that she had in her care a town of Roman status or a province, or both (Jolliffe, 1941).

The function of territorial goddess is further demonstrated by the fact that she holds a globe in her right hand indicating world-wide dominion. She has been elevated further, it seems and is now more than a localised, provincial goddess who gave her name to a tribe. She is according to this relief, divine protector of the world.

Brigantia has been connected by some writers with stone-worship in Yorkshire (Jolliffe, 1941). Such names as Bridestones are thought to indicate that she was the successor of the Bronze Age Mother Goddess of megalithic religion (Jolliffe, 1941). The Omphalos / sacred stone on the Birrens relief might be taken as further evidence for the continuity of stone-worship in northern Britain. It is possible that sacred stones associated with the cult of Brigantia may have been one reason for the identification with Caelestis of Carthage (Jolliffe, 1941) who we will meet later in this chapter. The stone is indicative of Juno Caelestis whose rule was world-wide. She was the embodiment of Syrian and African tutelary goddesses as well as being the consort of the almighty and all-powerful Jupiter Dolichenus. In other words, Brigantia is being assimilated by Caelestis, the former being regarded merely as the local manifestation of the latter (Fairless, 1989).

RIB 627

RIB 627 was found on an altar at Greetland. It is addressed to Victoria Brigantia and the Divinities of the Emperors and reads:

> Deae Victoriae Brigantiae\et Numinibus Augustorum\ Titus Aurelian\us dedit dedicavit pro se\et suis se magistro sacrorum
>
> *To the goddess Victoria Brigantia and to the Divinities of the two emperors, Titus Aurelius Aurelianus gave and dedicated (this altar) for himself and his family.*

The strength and power of Brigantia is witnessed in the appeal of the dedicant 'pro se et suis'. 'The concept implied of family protector is not far removed from that of healer' (Fairless, 1949). Two of the west Yorkshire altars were set up near the river Calder, Greetland 'was not far from the river' and Woodnook (RIB 628) was found in the river itself (Jolliffe, 1941). Her connection to water and its long-held association with healing is apparent once more in this description. If she is identified with Minerva, she is blended further with Sulis at bath and is healer of the hot springs.

RIB 1131

An altar at Corbridge is dedicated to Jupiter of Doliche, Caelistis Brigantia, and Salus. It contains the following wording:

> Iovi aeterno Dolicheno\et Caelesti Brigantiae\at saluti \ Gaius Iulius Ap\olinaris\centurio legionis VI iussu dei

> *To eternal Jupiter of Doliche and to Caelestis Brigantia and to health (or safety) set up by Salus Gaius Julius Apolinaris, centurion of the Sixth Legion, by order of the gods (or deities).*

Once more her role as healer is further evidenced in this relief by her association to the Roman Salus who is equated with Greek Hygieia, the Greek god of medicine (Jolliffe, 1941). On this relief she is also assimilated with Caelestis. Caelestis as we will later see was an African healing divinity and a cosmic goddess. The assimilation of African and Syrian deities at both Birrens and here at Corbridge is not random. Brigantia's prominence belongs to the reign of Severus and his son Caracalla. Severus was African in origin and his wife was Syrian (Jolliffe, 1941). It is said that Severus took preference to African rather than Roman deities (Tahar, 2008).

RIB 2066

The following inscription to Brigantia is found on an altar at Brampton:

> Deae Nymphae Brigantiae\quod voverat pro\salute et incolumitate\domini nostril invicti\imperatoris Marci Aureli Severi Antonini Pii felic(is) Aug(usti) totiusque domus divinae eius M.Coccieus Nigrinus (pr)oc(urator) Aug(usti) n(ostri) devo (tissim)us num(ini) maies}tatique eius v(otum) {s(olvit) l(ibens) m(erito)
>
> *To the Goddess the Nymph Brigantia, the vow which he had made for the welfare and safety of our invincible lord emperor M.Aurelius Severus Antoninus the Pious the Fortunate the August and of all his divine family, M.Cocceius Nigrinus, imperial commissioner of our August Emperor, consecrated to his divinity and majesty, paid willingly and deservedly.*

Addressed as the goddess Nymph she is yet again linked to water as a healing deity. A Nymph is a water deity and as we have gleaned, water and water bodies in general including wells and springs was often the setting for supernatural events (Fairless, 1989). The Brampton altar belonged to the reign of emperor Caracalla and makes reference to the emperor's health (Jolliffe, 1941). This could indicate that her name was on the lips of those that sought healing just like at Greetland (RIB 627).

RIB 1053

On an altar dedicated to Brigantia at South Shields we read the following:

> Deae Brigantiae sacrum Congennius V(otum) s(olvit) l(ibens) m(erito)
> *Sacred to the goddess Brigantia: Congennius willingly and deservedly fulfilled his vow.*

On the back of the altar is engraved a bird, on the right a patera and on the left side a jug. These are all elements which may represent the functions of fertility of the goddess. They could also represent healing. This inscription could also represent a mother goddess figure.

RIB 623

At Longwood, Slack, an altar dedicated to Bregans and the divinity of the emperor bears the inscription:

> Deo Breganti (sic) et num (inibus) Aug(ustorum) T.A(u)r(elius) Quintus d(ono) d(edit) p(ecunia) et s(umptu) s(uo)
> *To the God Bregans and the imperial divinities T.Aurelius Quintus gave (the altar) as a gift at his own cost and expense.*

Virtually nothing exists about this god in respect of his attributes and characteristics. We can only speculate that he was the consort of the goddess Brigantia and had the role of a multi-purpose tribal god. Further speculation might lead to the suggestion that the horned god so prominent in Brigantia, was a favoured aspect of this male god (Fairless, 1949). Maybe we can speculate that Bregans is the masculine form of Brigantia.

RIB Brit 53.55
At South Wiltshire Roman Temple, a curse tablet addressed to the god Bregneus reads:

> Deo Bregneo d(o) securim quam de hospitio meo Hegemonis perdidi..NAEVM inuolauit non (i)lli somnus nec sa(n)itas permittatu(r)....pertulerit usq(ue) ad tem(p)lum tuu)m) ut componimus P martulum quam prius perdidi eum quoque MV {.} NIT (traces) do?
>
> *To the god Bregneus I give the axe which I have lost from my house, (the house) of Hegemon. [...] has stolen, he is not to be permitted sleep or health (until) he has brought it to your temple as we ?arrange. The hammer which I previously lost, it also [...] ?I give.*

On inscriptions we see that dedicants were mostly men. They were men who were not born Roman citizens but were enfranchised by an emperor whose family name was Aurelius / Severi. On inscriptions we see an emphasis of their loyalty and duty which would be sensible if they were newly enfranchised natives (Jolliffe, 1941). Citizenship on provincials was to accelerate the Romanisation of a particular region. They were all sufficiently Romanised to honour their goddess through the Roman forms of cult. (Jolliffe, 1941).

Roman inscriptions have been invaluable in providing some evidence as to how Brigantia was regarded by her devotees. There are, however, as Hutton (2013) points out, loopholes within these pieces of evidence. The inscriptions feature mere names with no sense of context or function while the images of deities that have survived are mutilated or broken or features are dissolved by weathering (Hutton, 2013).

Although something is better than nothing, we really do need to rely on our own interpretation to get a sense of who Brigantia was / is. From what we may garner from Roman Inscriptions we can view Brigantia as a war goddess, a healing goddess, a tribal goddess, a celestial goddess and family protectress. She is comparable to Minerva and identifiable with Jupiter and Caelestis. She may be Celtic with Roman and Syrian undertones or she may be Roman with Celtic and Syrian undertones. Brigantia could also belong to neither cult, but instead be a blend of both. To get a clearer picture of who Brigantia is we can turn north now and meet the tribe, after whom she is named and who were possibly responsible for bringing Brigantia across the Irish sea into Ireland.

The Brigantes

Brigantia was eponymous goddess of the Brigantes (MacCulloch, 2014). The heartland of the Brigantes was in northern England and maps showing their territory show it stretching from east to west coasts. It covered the majority of the land between the River Tyne and the River Humber covering much of what is now Yorkshire, Northumberland, County Durham, Lancashire and into Cumbria. Known initially as Eburovices 'yew-conquerors' they were a large powerful tribe, territorially the largest Brythonic tribe or kingdom of ancient Britain. They would have had a wide trading influence, and chances are that their deities would have been known of and probably worshipped in neighbouring tribal areas. They were a restless race. Many of them probably emigrated to Ireland around 500 BC (Stanier, 1965, Stone, 2019).

Brigantes means 'high ones', Briganti means 'highest one'. The latter may be a designation for the Celtic Mother Goddess. (Ó hÓgáin, 2002). Their name may also be interpreted as meaning 'overlords' (Rivet and Smith, 1979). Regarding who they were, there are three possibilities:

- The Brigantes may have been a generic term used by the Romans for convenience to designate the people north of the Humber and Trent. This would mean the Celtic name 'Brigantes' would mean quite simply 'upland people'.
- The Brigantes may have been a name applied to most, if not all of various communities in Central Britain by themselves. This would have been meant they were all combined under a monarchy and chose for themselves the Celtic name most appropriate for folk belonging to an upland region.
- Another explanation might be that the Brigantes were a confederation of various tribal groups in which the Brigantes were the leading members. This could be that the Brigantes exercised or claimed an overlordship and it was because of this position that they were recognised by the Romans as the leading power of the region (Fairless, 1989).

As the tribe increased in importance and influence, it embraced other lesser communities within its orbit (Fairless, 1989). This has a feel of Brigid's expanding cloak. The population within Brigantian territory subdivided into distinct communities each with its own deities. Certain characteristics were common such as warrior-protector and woodland-hunter deities, watery contexts and connections to the cult of the head (Fairless, 1989). The concept of the horned god representing the woodland-hunter deity was special to the Brigantes (Fairless, 1989). These characteristics could have developed as a result of local conditions, for example, the hunter deity concept may have arisen amid a wooded environment and warrior deities may have resulted from differentiated communities needing to defend their own territories (Fairless, 1949).

From their initial encounter with the tribe, the Romans noted that they were ruled by a remarkable and powerful queen called Cartimandua. This is suggestive of the existence of such an aristocracy (Fairless, 1989). The occurrence of queenship among the Brigantes indicates the institution of descent through the female line (Fairless, 1989).

Cartimandua became a client ruler of Rome. As we saw earlier, Rome had dangled the carrot of luxury and sophistication to the Britons in an attempt to gain control and for the most part down South it had been successful. Cartimandua formed an alliance with Rome. In AD 48 a south-western section of her kingdom, rebelled and threatened the safety of a Roman official who was leading an expedition into Wales to overcome the king of the Catuvellauni tribe, Caractacus. He was king of the southern tribes who were still trying to resist Roman conquest. Caractacus attempted political asylum at Cartimandua's court but she handed him over to the Romans. Caractacus and his family were taken to Rome to be executed but his eloquence spared him his life. He managed to talk his way out of execution. He and his family were spared but they lived out the rest of their lives within the confines of Rome.

Cartimandua had married a British chieftain, Venutius. Once Caractacus had left the scene, Venutius was next in line for valour and military experience. However, within a few years Cartimandua had fallen out with Venutius. He was not her equal in kingship. When Venutius tried to raise an insurrection, Cartimadua enlisted Roman support. Her quarrel with Venutius was patched up and she remained dominant over the Brigantes. This fact, and her continued alliance with Rome, probably explains why the Brigantes did not join in the Boudiccan insurrection in AD 61. Eight years later their leader was once more quarrelling with Venutius. This time she divorced him. Venutius raised another insurrection and sent for neighbouring tribes outside the Brigantian confederation for help. Cartimandua requested Roman help once more which was granted. She and her new consort, Vellocatus were taken out of Brigantia, leaving Venutius as undisputed ruler of the Brigantes.

Venutius and the Brigantes were eventually defeated by the Romans and the whole of Brigantia came under Roman rule. It ceased to be a client kingdom and became just another area of Roman-occupied Britain. No more is heard of Cartimandua from this point on. The Brigantes, under Roman rule, started to move towards Ireland seeking political refuge. Ptolemy mentioned a group of Brigantes on the Wexford coast. In 1927 some excavations were carried out at Lambay island, off the coast of Co. Dublin which showed a cemetery of the period. Artefacts such as swords, shields and five Roman fibulae were all untypical of Irish weapons of the time but closer to the artefacts from cemeteries of the Iron Age in Brigantia (Ellis Beresford, 2013).

Back in Britain in about AD 118 or AD 117 the Brigantes rebelled and drove out or massacred the Roman legion which was stationed at York. The rebellion spread through North Britain. Hadrian arrived a year later bringing fresh troops and soon forced the Brigantes to surrender. Hadrian built his famous wall, with its periodic fortresses to provide a barrier against the Brigantes. It was a strong patrolled frontier, that marked the northern boundary of the Brigantes. All tribes to the north were considered Brigantia. It was built to keep them out but also, possibly to keep the southerners in (Stanier, 1965). The wall symbolised conquered Britain and those that opposed it (Stanier, 1965). The wall is 73 miles long and runs from west coast to east coast Britain near the present-day border between England and Scotland. With the extinction of the dynasty Brigantia may have lost something of her 'celestial' grandeur and her popularity with the Sixth Legion. The Romans have told us no more of her history (Jolliffe, 1941). Arguably, this could signify that Brigantia was indeed a Roman creation if she disappears as quickly as she rose to prominence. It could also mean, the wild, barbarian north and all associated therein was of no interest to the Romans, their goddesses such as Brigantia, included.

From the Brigantes tribe we can see Brigantia as symbolising unity amid the diversity within the region (Fairless, 1949). If we consider her a typical Celtic territorial goddess, she laid claim to the greater part of Central Britain as her domain. In time, away from the Roman spotlight and enforced warring associations, it is reasonable to imply that she expanded out across the Atlantic Ocean into Ireland bringing a specific aspect of her personality to the Emerald Isle in the form of Brigit / Brigid.

> There is certainly no good ground from dissociating the name Brigantes from the goddess Brigit, but if we suppose that the Irish people of that name were an off-shoot from the well-known people of the same name who stretched across Britain, north of the Humper and Mersey, we introduce a Brythonic element into Ireland which has not, I think, been hitherto recognised (Orpen, 1894).

Jolliffe (1941) is of a similar viewpoint:

> If all Brigantes were descendants of one Brigantian group, when they split up, their goddess must also have

done so, because the later forms of the cult would have been accommodated first to the geographical conditions of their respective areas and then to the experiences of their worshippers (Jolliffe, 1941).

This could be what MacCulloch (2014) posits, that Brigid was the *continuation* of the personality of Brigantia.

Brig

Across the Celtic tribes and nations are several deities by the same name with variations in spelling. Brig is found in Brigantia/Brigit / Brigid, Bricta of Luxeuil, Brigacaeia Matres, Brigindona of Gaul. Brig means high / exalted/ power/ force/ vigor/ flame (Nicholson, 1999) If the root of Brig is found in these goddesses, are we to assume that they were the same? Were they interchangeable or were they uniquely separate? We will look at several deities and see if there are any identifiable traits linking them to Brigantia or Brigid.

Bricta

At times a Celtic goddess is portrayed as part of a couple, either with a Roman or Celtic god. Sometimes it's hard to decipher who is the main deity and who is the consort. The pairing of the goddess to a male may simply be the representation of balance between male and female energies, resulting in fertility. At Luxeuil in the Saône valley of eastern France, there are remains of an ancient Celtic healing centre, combining hot springs and sanctuaries. Several deities appear to be referenced in the iconography at the site. At the Luxeuil site, Bricta is specifically identified as the consort of Luxovius, a god of healing and light which may be cognate with Lug. Iconography at Luxeuil depicts a sky-horseman bearing a solar wheel, a figure linked to Lug by many scholars. (Nicholson,

1999). Luxovius and Bricta are considered the local spirits of Luxeuil (Green, 2012). Little else is known about Bricta, 'although it has been suggested that she is linked to the Irish goddess Brigit, who became St Brigit when Ireland was Christianized' (Adkins & Adkins, 1996). The stem -Bri links her to Brigid even though in this pairing, it is Bricta who is the consort. Interestingly, Luxovius means light and he presides over a healing spring shrine. In time and in another country, it is Brigid who would preside over the domain of healing and be most associated with light. Based on Roman inscriptions we have evidence too of Brigantia as healer, namely through her water association.

Brigaciea Matres (Penalbo de Castro, Spain)

Brigantia is etymologically linked to the Matres Brigaecae, who are venerated in an inscription from Peñlba de Castro in Celtic Hispania (Beck, 2009). On an inscription we find the following wording:

> Ma(tribus) Brigaecis Laelius P{h}ainus V(otum) S(olvit) l(ibens) m(erito)
> *To the Mothers Brigeacae Laelius Phainus paid his vow willingly and deservedly'. (R.I.B).*

Brigindona / Brigindu

Brigantia is also related to the goddess Brigindona, honoured in a dedication engraved on a stone found in the (Gaulish) territory of the Aedui. The inscription is in Gaulish language and Latin lettering:

> Iccavos Oppianicnos ieuru Brigindon cantalon
> *Iccavos son of Oppianicnos offered (this) cantalon (pillar) to Brigindona.*

Brigantia and Belisama

Another goddess possibly linked to Brigantia is Belisama. Belisama is a goddess found in Gaulish inscriptions. Belisama is also likened to Minerva perhaps from 'qual' 'to burn' or 'shine' (MacCulloch, 2014). This is in keeping with the fire connection to Brigid as fire goddess and Brigantia through her assimilation with Minerva who was twinned with Sulis of Bath. There was a perpetual fire in the original spa at Aquae Sulis at Bath. Most things connected to heat and fire have always been linked to Brigid, so no wonder hot springs also attach themselves here. Belisama gave her name to the River Mersey, and many goddesses in Celtic myth are associated with rivers. With the name Belisama, I hear the superlative connection which although incorrectly spelt still gives the understanding of 'most', such as 'most bright/ 'most exalted' or indeed as per Ptolemy, Belisama is 'most warlike one'. Could the two concepts be a blend of most fiery and most warlike, meaning most destructible if we are to consider this through the lens of war?

Jolliffe groups Brigantia, Brigindu/ Brigindona and Brigit together. Worshippers of all three deities may have had common ancestors in the Briganti. In the period of Roman occupation of Britain, these goddesses would be sisters rather than identical (Jolliffe, 1941). Adaption to local conditions would have caused her to split into three distinct personalities. 'On the whole we are justified in assuming that Brig and the other abbreviations stand for Brigantiae' (Jolliffe, 1941).

Through the Roman inscriptions we have evidence to claim Brigantia as Celtic. There is also significant evidence to assume that she was a Roman creation, or more specifically a Severan creation. (Jolliffe, 1941). Because of the Roman Inscriptions we have found several epigraphic and iconographic references to her alongside Jupiter, Caelestis and Minerva. These were the three influences and associations from the classical world that were blended into an existing deity or that blended together to form Brigantia. By looking at these in detail we can perhaps strengthen our findings that we have already gathered or maybe even find new aspects of Brigantia's personality that needed the Roman spotlight in order to reveal herself.

Jupiter

Jupiter, whose cult is found in Britain by inscriptions from a number of military sites, was originally a Syrian god, the Ba'al ('Lord') of Doliche in Commagene (Joliffe, 1941). He was equated with Jupiter Optimus Maximus Capitolinus, the Roman sky-god and supreme protector of the Roman army. He is the most powerful of gods and father of the human race (Russell & Laycock, 2011). The majority of the dedications belong to the reigns of Severus and Caracalla. The cult had declined by about the middle of the 3rd century. Jupiter is generally portrayed as a bearded god, wearing the uniform of a Roman commander, brandishing a double axe and standing on the back of a bull. He is the supreme ruler of the universe. The fact that he was considered the supreme ruler of the universe denotes his greatness that was bestowed onto Brigantia. The consort of Jupiter was the goddess Ba'alat ('Lady'). Romanised as Juno Regina she was also Interpretatio Romana of Caelestis of Carthage.

Caelestis of Carthage

In addition to Jupiter Dolichenus, Brigantia was given the title Caelestis, which means she was identified with the main goddess of North Africa, the semitic Tanit. Tanit was Romanised as Dea Caelestis which means goddess of the heavens (Joliffe, 1941). Caelestis was the Semitic Tanit who, along with a male consort protected the city of Carthage. The cult of Tanit spread from Carthage to other Phoenician colonies in Africa and elsewhere. After Africa became a Roman province the Tanit-Cults became cults of Caelestis and continued to spread.

Local goddesses faded into the background at Carthage and Caelestis became the representative divinity of North Africa. At Carthage, under Roman rule she was Juno, outside Carthage she may have taken other forms (Joliffe, 1941). In her rawest essence she is the semitic fertility goddess called Astarte by the Greeks and Romans and interpreted by them as Aphrodite Urania and Juno Caelestis. Her distinctive aspect was the celestial. She was essentially a sky-goddess. She was believed to ride through the heavens on a lion. She was also a war-goddess, receiving the title of Victrix. Statues of victory stood in her shrine. One inscription refers to her breastplate. This shows her military side much like the Roman goddess Minerva. Astarte had a warrior type in some Phoenician colonies and there is evidence from North Africa of a Minerva wearing a mural crown. Joliffe (1941) asks if it is possible that the triple Jupiter Optimus Maximus, Juno Regina and Minerva Augusta were the Interpretatio of the warrior Caelestis and thus a Roman cult of two Caelestis originated, Juno and Minerva. She supports this from a dedication from Auzi in Mauretonia which begins as Caelestis Augustis. The link between Jupiter Dolichenus Caelestis Brigantia and Salus from the relief at Corbridge may be that they are all for this occasion divinities of healing (Jolliffe, 1941). Tanit had healing powers and retained them as Caelestis. Healing powers as we have found were also ascribed to Brigantia. This could have been because of her identification with Caelestia but maybe also because of her Celtic origin. If Brigantia has been identified with Caelestia, a cosmic goddess, she has been exalted to the highest rank of divinity. But it was customary for local goddesses to be regarded as manifestations of the greater divine powers. The assimilation of Brigantia to Caelestis was probably propaganda for the imperial cult, for in the Severan age the cult of cosmic powers is hardly separable from ruler-worship. Her cosmic character is corroborated by the art-type of the Birrens relief

(Jolliffe, 1941). The identification with Caelestis and the globe Brigantia carries shows that she was of sufficient importance in the eyes of the Imperial family to attach her into their own orbit for propaganda purposes (Jolliffe, 1941).

Minerva

Minerva often takes on the role of Celtic Mother Goddess since she has similar functions to those ascribed to Brigantia and Brigid as bringer of prosperity. Caesar lists Minerva as one of the main divinities of the Gauls. She is an early Italian goddess closely linked to warfare. Described as a solemn goddess of wisdom and strategic warfare she was invoked for arms and chivalry. Portrayals of Minerva show her winged, with the head of Medusa, crested, flowing-maned helmet, with Gorgon-headed aegis and spear (Gimbutas, 2001). She was the inspiration of the Trojan horse which was called the 'gift of Minerva' (Nelson, 1995). She was also the goddess who vented her wrath after the rape of Cassandra, the Trojan princess following the Trojan war. We saw a similar myth surrounding Boudicca. Minerva is said to be a descendent of an Indo-European battle-goddess and protector of kings and heroes. The root meaning of her name is connected to will, courage and fighting spirit (Nelson, 1995). Although a war-goddess in her own right she was also the warrior companion of Mars and is sometimes claimed to have been the wife of mars. Another aspect of her was *Minerva Medica*, patron of doctors. This healing aspect of her once again is a nod to Brigantia and very much with Brigid. Minerva is often portrayed exactly like Athena in both looks and personality. However, it has been argued that although there are overlapping similarities between the two, Minerva is a warrior goddess but is not also a goddess of handicrafts like her Greek complement, Athena.

Athena was the beautiful warrior goddess who protected her Greek heroes in battle. She was a master strategist, diplomat and protectress of cities and civilisations. She was renowned for her intelligence, practicality and her ambition (Murdock, 1990). These attributes were attributed to her during the Bronze Age (Gimbutas, 2001). Her mythology tells of how she sprang from her father, Zeus's head as a full-grown woman, wearing flashing gold armour, holding a sharp spear in one hand and dramatically announcing her arrival with a mighty war roar (Murdock, 1990). In her war-like tendencies, she is associated with the owl with which she can shapeshift. The owl naturally rules death and the underworld. She can also change into a vulture, a bird, most synonymous with death and decay. Athena was also the goddess of crafts. She invented the flute, trumpet, pottery, metallurgy, spinning and weaving as well as presiding over metal workshops. Before her specific war attributes, she was the mother of civilised life (Gimbutas, 2001). Brigid also became known for these three as healing, poetry and smithcraft.

Later the policy of Severus requiring that the Brigantes should be educated in the acts of peace and loyalty to the throne, she (Brigantia) was transformed into a Minerva, but a Minerva whose special care it was to watch over the safety and welfare of the emperors two sons, who were destined to succeed him and were conducting important military operations from a general headquarters in Brigantian territory (Jolliffe, 1941).

Based on the Roman inscriptions and the identification with Jupiter, Caelestis and Minerva we can certainly view Brigantia as a warrior goddess. 'The Romans appreciated her first as a battle goddess' (Jolliffe, 1941). She may be a sky goddess if she is likened to Caelestis. She may also be called a virgin warrior goddess if she is of Minerva and Athena. Although the traits of Jupiter, Caelestis and Minerva feature in the assemblage of Brigantia, it is Brigid with whom she shares significant semblances.

Brigantia and Brigid of Ireland

Brigantia was identical with the Irish goddess Brigit because Brigit was an almost universal Celtic goddess and a goddess of fertility and therefore a suitable heiress of the ancient Mother Goddess (Jolliffe, 1941). As already stated, MacCulloch views Brigid as the continuity of Brigantia in Ireland and states 'Brigit is thus the equivalent of the Gaulish goddess equated with Minerva by Caesar and found on inscriptions as Minerva Belisama and Brigindo' (MacCulloch, 2014). If we accept this, we can see many similarities between Brigid and Brigantia. Both have a reverence for the head; Brigantia's custom of head hunting in Celtic Britian and Brigid was associated with the head, for all matters of higher intellect. Pagan Celts believed that the soul dwelt in the head (Beresford-Ellis, 1995). There is a connection to oak with Brigantia and Brigid. There is evidence of wooden temples both in Britain and Gaul which acted as a focus point for religious rites and practices. In Christian myth Brigid founded her double monastery beneath an oak tree in county Kildare which means the church of the oak tree. Water for the cults of Brigantia and Brigid were important. Rivers were named after both Brigantia and Brigid and weapons were placed in rivers as offerings to her as goddess and the gods. Water was magical. It was the means to transport to another world and it contained healing properties such as in the holy wells of Ireland and in the thermal springs such as in Bath. Linked to Brigantia, Brigid became a deity in her own right (Stone, 2019). She emerged as a particular version of Brigantia. As encountered earlier with the Brigantes, her link is not only in name but also in the migration of the Brigantes from Britain to Ireland and also based on artefacts discovered in Ireland from the Brigantes (Stone, 2019, Ellis-Beresford, 2013).

Proof of the evolving nature of both Brigantia and Brigid exist. Brigantia started out as a local deity but soon spread out over the land in influence and name. Brigid too was initially associated with Leinster but soon became a national and transnational deity. Although we can see many similarities between Brigid of Ireland and Brigantia there is also a notable difference. Brigantia was associated with warfare as the tribal deity of the fractious and rebellious Brigantes and also because of her association with Minerva. As goddess, as we have already seen, Brigit is associated with warfare but in a small way. These warfare associations within Brigit are incomparable to the extent in which they exist within Brigantia.

With similarities and differences, I think we can attest that they both imbue similar energies. Although they are distinctly different. As we have come to know and love about Brigid, she is a deity that is fluid and always changing for whatever is needed of her. As a result, we could posit that Brigid evolved out of the deity Brigantia and came into veneration and prestige in Ireland for a different time and a different purpose.

Jolliffe (1941) does not see any connection between the two.

It is not necessary then to identify Brigantia with Brigit. It is more likely that they were goddesses of the same general type, exercising their powers, especially the power of healing, in accordance with the facilities provided by their environment (Jolliffe, 1941).

Influence of Other Classical Deities

Apart from the archaeological evidence on the inscriptions and the identification with Jupiter, Caelestis and Minerva and, of course, Brigid of Ireland, I think that we can view other classical deities playing a small role in her personality. As MacCulloch (2014) writes 'The stories and images connected with Brigit contain remnants associated with several goddess in Ireland and in parts of the ancient world, among them, Belisama, Juno, Isis, Vesta and Sul' (MacCulloch, 2014). There is some evidence of some of these deities in the personalities of both Brigantia and Brigid, in my opinion.

Fortuna
A Roman deity originally a fertility goddess identified with the Greek goddess Tyche. She was considered a goddess of fate, chance and luck. Fortuna's main symbol is the wheel, on which she is standing, possibly signifying instability. She is sometimes portrayed with a cornucopia and a rudder which may suggest steering the destiny of people. She is sometimes known as Fortuna of health and well-being or Fortuna the home bringer. These would have been particularly apt for troops fighting for the empire abroad wishing to return home safely. Within the character of Brigantia she can be seen to contain this energy.

Juno
Juno was named after the month of June and as we have seen is equivalent to the Greek goddess Hera. Besides being a supreme goddess, she was the goddess of light and moon, embodying all of the virtues of Roman Matron hood. Juno was for the Romans the goddess of marriage. As Juno Lucina, she became the goddess of childbirth and fertility. Brigid was renowned for childbirth and fertility. Juno was the midwife of ancient Rome. For this reason, Brigit is known as 'the Mary and Juno of the Gael' (Condren, 1989). Brigantia as sovereign tribal goddess is birther of tribes and victory for her people. As the land itself she represents fertility. The cow, perhaps the most sacred animal of Brigid of Ireland also featured in Roman mythology. Jupiter, Juno's husband had a wandering eye and is said to have turned a nymph with whom he was flirting into a cow when Juno arrived on the scene.

Juno was worshipped under various titles or epithets; 'she who leads the bride into marriage', 'she who leads the bride to her new home', 'she who loosens the bride's girdle', 'bringer of light', 'goddess of fruit'. 'matron of honor', 'bone setter' or 'bone strengthener'. She was also known as 'Juno protector of spearmen and was said to have been worshipped in each of the thirty military and political administrative units of Rome. A prayer to her includes 'Juno Curtis, protect my fellow natives of the curia with your chariot and shield'. Another title for her was 'one who warns'. In mythology her sacred geese had warned of an impending attack by the Gauls. In yet another title she is Juno Populonia meaning of the people and also of infantry. The army was made up of the common people who were called to arms. As such she was goddess of soldiers. Her other titles included goddess of protection, protector of the state and of girls at puberty (Adkins & Adkins, 1996). Light bringer and healer are all connected to Brigid. Juno was for the Romans, but of fire in a destructive way. He became identified with the Greek god, Hephaestus, the Greek god of metal working and played a significant and vital role in equipping the empire's army. Fire and blacksmithing were two very strong attributes of Brigid. There may possibly be a link back to Juno and her son Vulcan for this particular association.

Victoria

Two inscriptions bear the name victory. Victory-Brigantia interestingly, is not found outside Yorkshire. Victory was a goddess of the Roman armies and the equation of Brigantia with Victoria might well have been made by soldiers at the time of the revolt or in older wars against the Brigantes. She was an important deity for the Romans and appears regularly on coinage from the late third century BC. She came to be regarded as the guardian of the empire and her altar in the Senate house in Rome became a symbol of paganism (Adkins & Adkins, 1996). She was popular with the army and had a special connection with various legions and later with several emperors. Her statue was one of the most famous in Rome. On her altar of victory, senators burned incense, offered prayers annually for the welfare of the empire, took their oaths and pledged allegiance on the accession of each new emperor (Sheridan, 1966). We see a connection between Brigantia and the Roman goddess Victoria. Victoria was the personification of victory, who was central to Roman ideology as patroness of war. Victoria also brings peace and prosperity (Swan, 2019). Peace and prosperity were two major characteristics of Saint Brigid.

Vesta

The Roman goddess Vesta was a goddess of the hearth and home, which were both private and public. Vesta developed from a fusion which took place in central Italy between the fire worship of the Indo-European pastoralists who migrated into the region during the fourth millennium BC and of the worshippers of the great Earth Goddess who predated their arrival by about two thousand years. Vesta was a unique deity for many reasons. She, unlike other Roman gods and goddesses did not have a public image that was presented in public and private sanctuaries. She remained abstract, represented by the hearth fire only (Wright, 1995). Vesta's sanctuary was round in shape while other temples were quadrangular. The circle is a symbol of the goddess. All the power of the goddess is on earth. The earth and hearth were symbols of the home. Brigantia may thus be the earth and Brigid the fire wherein resides the energy of Vesta.

Chapter 4

Connecting with Brigantia

Journey to Hadrian's Wall

My sense of Brigantia, is that she is first and foremost a goddess of the land. To connect to her essence, I wanted to travel to a place associated with her. As her tribe, the Brigantes were the ones considered barbarian and were segregated from the conquered, more civilized south, I felt the spirit of her tribe in the North of England was as good as place as any to get a feel for her. I had hoped that the land of Northumberland and Hadrian's Wall would feel like an energetic tug of war laying claim to her and I would instinctively know which side was justified.

What struck me the most about this land, were the impressive rolling hills dotting the landscape. These, to me, had a very striking and symbolic presence. The hills made me think of Russell & Laycock (2011) who write 'these important contour-hugging enclosures seem to provide confirmation of the warlike nature of Iron Age society, which we are told by Roman writers such as Julius Caesar, was always feuding, brawling, fighting and stealing' (Russell & Laycock, 2011). Were these hills symbolic of Brigantia? Did these hills emanate such a sacred power that they named their beloved goddesses after them? Did they represent such stark protection during battle that they were considered divine?

Gazing at the landscape I was reminded of the stem of her name -brig and how it means 'high', either elevated, exalted or indeed both. I found myself gazing up and imagining myself living in such a warring culture that I would turn to these mighty hills and invoke my goddess for protection and assistance. Standing, looking at the hills I marvelled at their sheer height and vastness. They indeed, must have been considered majestic and all deities connected to them must have, in addition, been considered grandiose. In their association with war and protection, I could only feel Brigantia to be synonymous with this and to feel her as not only a Celtic goddess of the land but without a doubt a war goddess.

What was astonishing about Hadrian's wall is its length of 73 miles. A striking feature of the wall is that it is done with dry stone. For the Celts, this would have been the first time for them to observe the skill of masonry. Perhaps the construction of the wall was not only to keep the wild barbarians of the north out but maybe to try and impress them to the potential powers of the Romans and what greatness, Roman allegiance might bring to their lives.

Looking at temple remains at Vindolanda where both local and Roman gods and goddesses were worshipped struck a chord. The Romans were most probably very deliberate in their openness to local deities. As Russell and Laycock (2011) say 'a society whose religious beliefs are not persecuted is far less likely, perhaps to rebel'. 'A conquering power must, if it is to prove successful and maintain control, accept all local religions, or modify them only gently' (Russell & Laycock, 2011). This is somewhat reminiscent of the Christian approach arriving in Ireland and their gradual assimilation of pagan practices into their own, as well as integrating a key goddess to Saint, Brigid. Slowly and gently with smiles and open arms of acceptance, original practices become diluted and retain a mere fraction of themselves.

It was not surprising really that I chose Hadrian's wall to see if Brigantia felt more Roman or Celtic as here was where the two worlds associated with her met. Throughout my time there I constantly thought of Brigit the goddess being assimilated into Brigid the Saint. If this gradual assimilation of Brigid from goddess to Saint could happen in Ireland, then it is entirely plausible that this was not the first time. It is possible that her predecessor, Brigantia, was also blended from local Celtic goddess into the Roman pantheon. Her energy has been a constant current that flows and flourishes, only to retreat and flow in a new direction once again. Even if she was considered a malleable force in imperial hands her time in the spotlight was quite short. In the aftermath of Roman rule her energy would flow once more to Ireland where she would undergo another series of transmutations and continue to flourish for centuries. During this time, she would rise and retreat in popularity as goddess and saint but her presence would always be felt. It is possibly thanks to the Romans that she did flourish as Brigid and possibly it is thanks to the Romans that we can work our way backwards and uncover the Celtic Brigantia that existed before their arrival and from whom all Brigids might have come.

Now that we have some background information I'd like to offer my own individual animals, colours and symbolism that I personally connect to Brigantia. I have felt these to be pertinent to the personality of Brigantia from Roman inscription imagery and from their depiction of her, as well as from my intuitive perspective. In your own journey with Brigantia, you may feel these, or you may not. The following reflect my point of view, only.

Animals

'To the Celts animals were special and central to all aspects of their world' (Green, 2002) For the Celts there was a strong link between animals and the supernatural. Animals were the mediators between the gods and humankind. The Romans humanised their gods and goddesses, whereas the Celts, much to the amazement of the Romans saw their gods in animals. The Celtic perception of gods in body form took on the features of beasts, such as hooves, horns and antlers. Artists exaggerated or enhanced particular features of the animal to highlight the aesthetic quality. Because of the proximity of the natural world to rural communities, the Celts had a direct reliance on the land, crops and especially on animals. They depended on domestic animals for their livelihood, on wild animals for hunting and fur and on horses especially for warfare. Brigantia, similar to the beast is wild, untamed and free in her expression of the Celtic goddess. She is the realm of earth itself, found in the mountains, moors, boglands, forests, streams, rivers, ponds and oceans. Her spirit is one of liberty and expansion found in the smallest, wildest and fiercest of creatures but most especially I think, in the following animals:

Bird: On an inscription in South Shields, Arbeia, Brigantia wears a bird on her back. At Birrens there are wings and a plumed helmet. Anything bird-like which had the aerial view for battle and the ability to rise above the enemy in victory. Reference with the bird for all things high can be associated with Brig.

A bird in flight can be viewed as embodying the very meaning of her name, 'high'. Waterbirds even more so, as they inhabit both land and water, so are intrinsically liminal, and dual. They are the travellers between the earthly plane and the celestial skies. The oystercatcher is particularly related with Brigid in Scotland. In Scottish Gaelic, it is named 'Bridein' ('Gille Brid'), which means 'Bride's bird' or 'servant of Bride' (Daimler, 2016). The oystercatcher is a shore bird, so naturally dwells often at that liminal space between sea and land. It is also black and white with a long, bright red beak. Other birds associated with Brigid include the linnet, known as 'bigein Bride', and the skylark. In Ireland, to have heard the lark's song on Imbolc morning was a lucky sign that good things were to come throughout the year. The swan features in Celtic lore, most notably in the *Children of Lir*, and is associated with shapeshifting. It is seen as a guide between the worlds too. Again, we see the themes of reinventing and in-betweenness that are so often connected with Brighde. Since the swan can both swim and fly, they embody the water while being able to reach the sun. Interestingly, water and solar symbolism are closely linked to healing cults (Green, 2011). The colour of the swan can be linked to chastity and purity too, which certainly echoes the virtuousness of Saint Brigid. The 'long phallic neck' and 'protruding posteriors', as Gimbutas writes (1991), 'depict a form not quite human but a hybrid of a water bird and a human female'. Free as a bird is a saying depicting its ability to fly free and escape the constrictions of earth. This is in keeping with the wild, free energy of Brigantia.

Boar: The boar was often adopted as a battle emblem (Green, 2002). The boar is naturally a shy animal but is considered a. It is aggressive, determined, strong and destructive and rushes headlong into action. It lives wild in forests and is symbolic of courage and strength, especially if cornered. The boar is a perfect animal of Brigantia that represents the ability to fight back, even if not naturally aggressive.

Goose: On a statuette of a war-goddess in Brittany, the goddess wears a goose-crested helmet. The goose 'is a potent symbol of war, aggression and guardianship' (Green, 1997). In central and Eastern Europe, geese were frequently buried with warriors as well as battle equipment and pork. Like pork, geese could provide food and also like pork, geese were a war symbol (Green, 2011). Caesar mentions the goose as a taboo, non-edible creature that was maybe too sacred to consume (Green, 2011). Described as belligerent, fierce, aggressive and alert, it is a perfect symbol for Celtic war deities such as Brigantia.

Horse: Horses transformed methods of warfare. Through their ability to cover vast ground warriors were able to go to battle quicker. Horses were mounts for warriors and warrioresses. Male and female warriors and charioteers were frequently found on Celtic coins. They also had the ability to pull funerary wagons to the tombs of the high-ranking dead (Green, 2002). On Celtic farms horses were used for rounding up herds and were a symbol of pastoral wealth, as is still the case today. Although horses are not traditionally aggressive, stallions can be trained to bravely face their opponent using their teeth and hooves in combat. Undoubtedly, the neighing of horses flying into battle would have been a deliberate war tactic to cause panic and terror. When considering the energies of Brigantia, an image of a wild mare free riding through the lands on a horse easily comes to mind. The horse as transport can take you to new lands as was the case with the wandering Celts. Working like a horse, transforming and cultivating the land for survival and protection is in keeping with the mother goddess, Brigantia, as protectress of her people. The horse also featured in the history of Boudicca. On horseback she was able to round up and unite tribes with her speech and lead forces into battle.

Serpent: Perhaps no other animal has been vilified as much as the serpent. The serpent has become the absolute enemy of humankind. It has been associated with the most despicable of feminine traits; sultry, charming, teasing, fluid, enchanting, suffocating, captivating.

We see the snake connection to Brigantia in the Roman inscriptions of Britain found at Adel. Athena, as a blend of Brigantia, was descended from the bird and snake goddess, was so renowned for protectress of the community and sustainer of life (Gimbutas, 2001). These two attributes are also found in Brigantia. During the Neolithic, portrayals of the snake goddess consistently featured a crownlike headpiece. Crowns symbolised wisdom and wealth. The crowned snake is the queen (Gimbutas, 2001).

Stag: The stag is regularly found in the various Celtic cultures as a powerful symbol of virility, and authority. As such, the stag is representative of clan heritage and is in resonance with Brigantia, tribal goddess of the Brigantes. The stag is the pride of the forest and has a jaw-dropping, commanding, majestic presence. Renowned for their speed, strength and wisdom and virility, the stag embodies the entire forest through its antlers which can be viewed as his royal crown. The regal essence of the stag is akin to Brigantia and her queen like energies. The stag is an animal that commands respect. Gently emerging into sight, the apparition-like presence of the solitary stag captivates the watcher to the point of tears at the almighty sight. The stag often arrives in meditations or journeys to the otherworld as a way-shower or advice-giver. He is the gateway between this world and the next. As an animal of Brigantia we can see the royal like connection but we can also see the connection of the stag to warfare. The stag is particularly aggressive during the rutting season.

Swan: In the later Bronze Age, swans appear on Urnfield metalwork, constantly associated with sun-symbols (Green, 2011). Swans can swim and fly, and they also feature in many Irish legends. The swan, in my opinion, is representative of metamorphosis. Brigantia has altered and evolved to include many features of her classical sisters. The swan, by its very nature is also fiercely protective of its young and is quick to react, making it an appropriate symbol of Brigantia. In my Priestess training in Glastonbury, we associate the swan with the north direction. Able to fly most high, touching back to the stem -Bri (in both Brigantia and Brigid, and representing air, the swan is most befitting for Brigantia. However, I see the swan as an animal of Brigantia for another reason. The swan is always described as serene, elegant and a beauty to behold. She is graceful and feminine and gently glides through the water. What we don't immediately notice is the furious peddling beneath the water's surface. What we don't always notice when watching from afar is the quick defence to a breach of boundary and what we don't always acknowledge, is that a thing of exquisite beauty can quickly turn angry and cause hurt. Just because it's pretty to look at, does not mean it is not capable of standing its ground and fighting back when provoked.

Colours

Blue: Royal blue, the very name itself indicates royalty. A deeper shade of blue and not yet dark enough to be navy, royal blue was created for a competition to make a robe for Queen Charlotte, consort of King George III. When they won, the business in that invented the dye received a certificate to sell it under the name. An intense and vivid colour, royal blue indicates authority, trust and confidence. It is also a colour I most associate with authenticity, like the blue flame of a fire, it is closest to the source. Superior and powerful, royal blue has long been associated with rulers and monarchs in British history. The cultivation of woad in England and some parts of Europe helped many towns become rich. The dye was expensive to produce and not dependable. As such it was used by the wealthy and became associated with nobility. Such a deep colour, is most befitting for Brigantia, for the Queen of the Brigantes. As part of the union jack, blue represents a sense of patriotism which we find with Brigantia as protectress of her territory. Blue was also the colour the Picts painted on themselves and also of the Celts in battle. Whether the colour was intentionally blue, or all they had, we don't know. But possibly it was an effort to bring down the power of the celestial heavens above them for battle and to embody the protection of their goddess Brigantia.

Gold: Another colour most in keeping with the sovereignty of Brigantia is gold. Gold was very much connected to Athena, who as we have seen, is the equivalent of Minerva, who both form a part of Brigantia's identity. Athena is said to have been wearing flashing gold armour when she was birthed. Gold is also indicative of royalty but also signifies achievement and triumph. The rich colour obviously depicts wealth and reminds us of Cornucopiae, another symbol of Brigantia. Gold is in addition, a colour of knowledge which once more, links to Athena for her strategic planning and also to Brigid, for her intellect. Gold inspires high elevated spirituality and a deep understanding of ourselves which mostly comes into full force in our queen years and our golden years. Gold is commonly associated with prestige, honour and influence. No wonder to win a gold medal is such an honour. A colour of high status, it is appropriate for the crowned goddess Brigantia.

Symbols of Brigantia

Armour: Steel armour which usually represents Athena or Minerva is a mode of protection that typically denotes resilience, durability and strength in combat. Brigantia as protectress of her land and tribe can be invoked through armour memorabilia or images of armour.

Arrow: The arrow is a tool of war and connected to Athena and Brigantia. The fiery arrow is often associated with Brigid of Ireland for inspiration or healing. For Brigantia, the fiery arrow was instrumental in starting combat. Volleys of spears were thrown at the start of an engagement as an important first stage of combat (Green, 2012). The arrow as a symbol indicates the conscious pursuit of one's ideals and goals, the purposeful direction of one's energy. This is most appropriate for Brigantia as a symbol.

Chariot: The chariot was of huge importance to the warring Celts. Such were their importance that they have been found in burials along with the warrior. The chariot was not used in the heat of battle but as a means of arriving to action. The warriors were a frightful sight and sound as they hurtled along at speed, erect and standing tall. The clattering wheels and hooves along with shouting and roaring as well as beating their shields was used to it's full to terrify the enemy. One person drove, another threw spears and then jumped out to fight. The chariot represents communal support, combat and solidarity which are all contained within the essence of Brigantia.

Cornucopia: At Corbridge Brigantia is depicted with a cornucopia. The cornucopia is a curved, hollow goat's horn or a similar shape that overflows with fruit and vegetables. Cornu copine, meaning horn of abundance or known more commonly as 'The Horn of Plenty'. The cornucopia was found on many motifs in classical Greek and Roman mythology. It became associated with deities associated with the harvest, prosperity, or spiritual abundance such as Fortuna who is blended into the image of Brigantia. It is also suggestive of untamed sexual vigour and life itself. Isis, as we have seen was the great mother goddess and is also a component of the persona of Brigantia. She was often portrayed with corn showering down between cow's horns and is known as the 'Mother of corn' (Birnbaum, 2001). Isis was integrated into Roman life and featured on Roman coinage. Interestingly, she was also absorbed with the Roman goddess Fortuna.

Crown: Brigantia is crowned like a tutelary deity at Birrens. There is no symbol of queendom quite like that of the crown. As we saw with the crowned serpent, the crown is significant of wisdom and wealth and denotes power and protection over one's tribe. The crown enables one to know all, to see hidden treasures, and to understand the language of animals (Gimbutas, 2001). As a land goddess, this is in keeping with Brigantia. Her mural crown suggests that she had in her care a town of Roman status or a province or both at once (Jolliffe, 1941).

Globe: The globe is generally a symbol of interconnectedness. From the perspective of the great mother goddess, we are all her children, even with different languages and customs. Within Brigantia, the two worlds, Celtic and imperial simultaneously exist. To hold up the globe is to see the diversity of humankind and yet to see the similarity in us all. The globe as a visual representation of the earth enables one to condense the smaller details of planning and to see the bigger picture. The shape of the globe as a sphere is also indicative of the cycle of life that is death and rebirth. As well as all of the above, the globe is a symbol of victory, most associated with Minerva, a façade of Brigantia. As Brigantia is an authority icon, the globe as a symbol of her can remind us that we have the world in the palm of our hands once we step into our power.

Hill Forts: High up on hill tops, hill forts represent the defence and protection of communities and tribes against attack. Hill forts are a powerful symbol of Brigantia who was the defender and protector of her people. They also represent the close proximity between humankind and the gods, goddesses.

Horns: Throughout the military zone of Northern Britain, many horn representations are found. Both male and female horned figurines represent aggression, fertility, ferocity, power and strength (Green, 2011). Female horned figurines appeared at Icklingham, Suffolk and Richborough. Horns were given to certain gods at certain times to increase the power of their symbolism. Horns are the spiritual antennae to the unseen world. They are also a symbol of death and rebirth as they are shed in winter and regrown in Spring. The Celts often bestowed animal attributes to both humans and gods (Green, 2011). Interestingly, I see another triadic form here. Horns represent and bind the human-god-animal triad. Attributes of all three interchange and blend into one another. Brigantia, as sovereign goddess of the

Brigantes is in the Otherworld, is within the fighting warrior, and without, in the land beneath their feet. Wild, untamed and horned is how I sense Brigantia.

Shield: The shield has long been a symbol of protection and shelter which are, of course, under the remit of Brigantia. It also is a powerful means of demonstrating no. No to coercion, no to retreat, no to surrender.

Spear: The spear was originally a weapon of personal protection against wild animals. It symbolises courage, power and striving, all of which are connected to Brigantia. In Greek mythology, which had an influence on the personality of Brigantia, the spear represented wisdom and strategy which were essential for victory in war. The spear is one of Minerva's symbols. The spear also, to me makes a statement of making a claim for what you want. It is narrowing the selection and laying claim to something. When done for the highest good, the spear is an important symbol.

Sword: The sword is one of the strongest symbols of swift action. Linking the sword to Queen Brigantia, one can almost hear 'off with his head'. The sword helps cut old ties to people, places, things and creates a blank canvas for new beginnings. The sword symbolises active living, active choices and responsibility for one's path. Often encrusted with jewels and expensive crystals it is the weapon of royalty fit for a queen to use for the good of her people.

Water: In ancient Rome, water was worshipped like a deity. Its abundance not only meant the wellbeing of Rome's citizens but was also a sign of wealth and power for its burgeoning civilisation. Water as a healing source, such as the waters at the Roman spa in Bath, which came to be associated with Brigantia.

Many of the pilgrims that came to Bath were women as per archaeological remains found such as hair-pins, spindles and model breasts. Doctors attended the spa too curing in particular gout and arthritis which became a common reason to visit the spa. Water was sacred and represented liminal space where the supernatural meets the earthly. Water was a gateway that closely bound water and healing and especially healing and thermal springs. Water represented purification and a life force and where springs were hot, the curative power was intensified (Green, 1997). The tradition of endowing wells with supernatural power is at its commonest immediately before the Roman period (Green, 2011). Minor deities dwelled in lakes bog rivers, springs and wells but the rivers Brent in England and Braint in Wales which we know are named after her, suggest her significance (Ross, 1997).

Wheel: In the context of Brigantia and the Brigantes, the wheel on the chariot was instrumental as a war accessory. The Celts relied on the chariot as well as the horse to go into battle. Symbolically, the wheel represents setting things in motion, taking the wheel, moving forward. It also enables one to move on to pastures new, like the Celts, moving on to and conquering new lands. In moving into new lands such as Ireland, they may have brought the worship of their goddess Brigantia with them.

The wheel was also a sun symbol and featured on stone carvings and coinage all over Europe, most probably copied from the Greek and Romans. The wheel with the centre as the sun and the spokes indicating rays is linked to Rome's almighty god figure, Jupiter. Miniature wheels were worn as talismans and were buried with the dead. Miniature wheels were symbolic of the sun which had been venerated as a specific deity in pre-Celtic and even pre-Roman times. Sun-wheels were linked to the cult of fertility and the Celtic mothers. Most probably because of the influence of the Great Mother Goddess Isis, who was often portrayed wearing a sun disk on her head and was known as the bringer of light (Birnbaum, 2001). The sun connection, Brigid as bringer of Spring / light may have evolved from Brigantia through the Brigantes who had been influenced by Roman religious belief.

To intentionally connect to Brigantia, I suggest rooting yourself on the ground to feel her through the sacred land where you find yourself. Setting up an altar using the above-mentioned symbols, images, or colours or indeed others of your own choosing can help strengthen your instinct as to what she represents for you. In the next chapter I have listed all the issues that I think are best suited for Brigantia's expertise. Once again, the list is entirely subjective and reflects what I have gleaned from my research and my own intuition.

Chapter 5

What Does Brigantia Stand For?

Brigantia, in my opinion, is a specific face of Brigid that can assist with issues pertaining to the following:

Action: When ideas come rushing in and emotions well up in support of a cause, then action is the essential step in making your mark to fight for your cause. Call upon Brigantia to put fire in your belly and fear to the side as you brave your path like Boudicca.

Authority: Call upon Brigantia to enable you to see your relationship to authority from your childhood and how it has shaped you to date in holding your own power. If there are issues relating to authority and your perception of authority, ask for her to pave the way to the most suitable therapist to begin your healing journey.

Boundaries: Establishing boundaries and sticking to them requires a belief in self and self-respect. Call upon Brigantia for help with recognising, who or what is overstepping the mark and for assistance in creating your circle of protection.

Change: When we crave change our soul is ready for a new experience. Change in its ideal form makes us giddy and expectant of good things to come. But actual change, of moving home, location, job or leaving friends or a partner can open the floodgates of fear. Call upon Brigantia for help with moving forward, learning and growing as a person.

Earth: As protectress of our sacred earth, call upon Brigantia for all issues related to sustainability and to the environment.

Empowerment: Call upon Brigantia to show you a vision of your most powerful self. Where are you? What are you doing? In order to become this version of yourself you need a vision. With this vision in mind, you can begin to take baby steps to reaching that potential.

Equality: For any sense of gender inequality call upon Brigantia to help you remember the strength of the divine feminine power. Remember the women of Gaul and their warring roles alongside men and remember the power and strength of Boudicca.

Fearlessness: Call upon Brigantia to face any of your fears in stepping in to your power. Fears might include possibly starting a war by speaking your truth, establishing boundaries, saying yes to a new experience, or saying no to certain demands. It may also be in speaking up for a person or cause or taking action on behalf of a person or a cause.

Healing: Brigantia demands of us to step up into our power by healing our relationship to authority. By reconciling breaches of fear of authority we inevitably empower ourselves and enter into our own sovereign state.

Leadership: For all types of leadership or growth opportunities call upon Brigantia to fearlessly take the bull by the horns and grow into who you are meant to be.

Lifeforce: To feel the very life force of the scared earth and all of her glorious inhabitants that includes: animals, vegetation, plants, rocks and minerals call upon Brigantia to remind you of your divine place on earth and your responsibility to protect all life forms here.

Masculine Energy: To heal our relationship with the masculine energy within us all ask Brigantia to guide you to a healer or therapist that can help you undo patriarchal conditioning or to heal relationships to males in your life or family.

Maturity: Maturity goes hand in hand with authority. It is no surprise that our queen years come after the childbearing years when life experience and wisdom is substantial. Call upon Brigantia for help in making decisions that are based in fairness, maturity and that reflect wisdom that comes with age and experience.

Menopause: With the reset and change in our bodies at Menopause there is a time for a new beginning. The new beginning comes with an understanding and appreciation that a significant part of our lives is over and now is the time to prioritise ourselves and our desires.

Migration: We have all come from migrants, from the earliest Homo Sapiens from Africa to the migrating Celts. For help with moving solo or as part of a group to new lands call upon Brigantia for protection and safety.

National Pride: Call upon Brigantia for remembering your country's past that has helped shape what it is now and to appreciate all that former inhabitants went through in order for you to be here at this exact moment in time with all that you have.

No: For help in saying no and meaning no, call upon the spirit of Brigantia.

What Does Brigantia Stand For?

Politics: For all things political and relevant to humanity's experience at local, national and global level invoke Brigantia for a better understanding and for inspired action on how best to be an active citizen on a local, national or global level.

Protection: Brigantia as ultimate protectress of her people is the perfect spirit for help when feeling unsafe. Call upon Brigantia when you need to feel protected or when you wish for protection for others and the world at large.

Queendom: Honouring you self and your gifts of purpose places you high on your throne of power. For help in remembering your authentic, queen self, call upon Brigantia.

Rebellion: When in need of facing up to and pushing back against established doctrine and regulations that place humanity at war with each other call upon Brigantia.

Self-awareness: Call upon Brigantia for help with understanding your life to date and who you are essentially. With this knowledge will come a passion and a zest for your cause that will overcome any other fears that hold you back.

Sovereignty: To be sovereign is to be accountable and responsible for all the decisions you make in your life. Call upon Brigantia for help with knowing thyself and unapologetically to yourself and others for forging ahead with that path.

Strategic Planning: To get an overview of a situation or issue, call upon Brigantia to assist with the bigger perspective and the careful planning of details for a victorious outcome. Contained within Brigantia is the Athenan/ Minervan energy who are considered experts in organisation and strategic planning.

Strength: Call upon Brigantia to become stronger physically, emotionally and mentally. This may start with getting help form an expert in one or all three of these domains. Only by improving yourself in mind, body and spirit can you be at your best to ride into battle and bring about the change you were born to make.

Tribal connection: Call upon Brigantia for help in finding your tribe or keeping your tribe connected and safe.

Unity: Invoke Brigantia for help with finding your tribe or for help with finding deep, meaningful connection in person in a digital world. Invoke Brigantia just like Boudicca did in unifying the sheer number of people to fight for what you believe in.

Valour: For calling it out, standing your ground or instigating protest or action against injustice call upon Brigantia.

Vision: For help with envisioning your life and the world we want to live in call upon Brigantia to help get a clear picture and most importantly take action to bring the vision to life.

Wild woman: The wild woman is a strong essence of Brigantia. She is happiest barefoot on the land, listening to the birds, connected to nature in all its forms and in sync with the natural world. Untamed and free she is a free spirit. When we embody the wild woman of Brigantia, we strip away noise, materialism and all that doesn't speak to our soul. In our rawest essence, we will not hold our tongue. We will not shut up. We will not know our place. We will stand tall. We will heed our inner calling and charge forth on our mission like the mighty Boudicca.

Conclusion

We are at the end of our journey with Brigantia, for now. She emerged from the hilltops of northern England and allowed us to catch a glimpse of her. I think it is fair to say that we are all the richer and wiser from our time with her. The answers I had hoped to get from our encounter feel more solid, in my mind anyhow. My reason for embarking on this journey with Brigantia was to see if the Brigantes came to Ireland and if they did, did they bring their goddess Brigantia with them. I feel the answer to this is yes. From several sources (Ellis Beresford, 2013, MacCulloch, 2014 and Ptolemy) we can claim that there is evidence of the Brigantes tribe coming to Ireland. I had hoped to ascertain if Brigantia was the predecessor of Brigit/Brigid. I didn't find the answer categorically, but I get a sense that there are grounds to argue this. Brigantia and Brigit could not be the same goddess. Jolliffe (1941) states that Brigantia belongs to a few years of a Romano-British period but the evidence for Brigit comes from Irish literature of a much later time. This proves that they did not exist simultaneously but if we hold onto the idea that Brigit, has and is a blended energy then we can possibly agree with MacCulloch (2014) that Saint Brigid was the continuation of Brigantia. Stone (2019) also supports this by claiming that Brigid is linked to Brigantia but became a deity in her own right. Brigid emerged as a particular version of Brigantia (Stone, 2014). The war aspect of Brigantia did not feature very much with Brigit, but it is there, nonetheless.

Perhaps the most pertinent question I had was whether Brigantia could be claimed Celtic or Roman? I agree with Salway (1967) who says that although she flourished and gained prominence under Roman rule, the various aspects of her personality indicate the presence of a Celtic divinity beneath the façade of Romanisation. I think there is too much evidence to argue for the existence of a local goddess before the arrival of Rome. One reason is that linguistically her name meaning 'most high' is connected to the hilltops of northern England, to the land held so sacred by the Celts. She is also connected to water veneration and healing which was a Celtic custom. Brigantia is also a Gaulish goddess. Mentioned earlier is a statuette in the Museum of Brittany, Rennes presumed to be that of Brigantia. We can, in fact, make a good case for Brigantia coming into Britain by the Gauls, if indeed, she was not already a deity of Britain.

Although we can appreciate her Celtic origins, there is no denying the Roman influence on the personality of Brigantia. Through the various goddesses bearing her name and even those that don't, we can see how the specific impact of these goddesses contributed to the façade of Brigid known as Brigantia and possibly later in the development of the Saint Brigid in Ireland, Wales and Scotland. The Romans had a significant impact on Gaul which resulted in Gaulish goddesses also losing their distinct personalities. But even with Roman influence, we can see the association of healing and light from her presence as Bricta and Sul. As Brigindo we see her familiar traits of healing, crafts and fertility. The fire of Brigid is found in Belisama and also in Vesta. Prosperity and good luck are seen in Fortuna. Childbirth and fertility are found in the characteristics of Juno. Protector of the home and empire are discovered in the make-up of Victoria. Isis, the Great Mother bestows us with magic, fertility, the moon symbol and the cow's horn all associated with the goddess Brigid.

I believe Brigantia belongs to both the Celtic and the Roman world. Why the Romans blended local deities still remains unknown (Zoll, 1995). Maybe it was to assert their power as Webster (1995) suggests or maybe it was a cunning ploy to imply amicability (Russell & Laycock, 2011). Whatever their reasons, as per two Roman inscriptions (at South Shields and Brampton)

Conclusion

where the dedicant is specifically claiming to have honoured his vow, Brigantia was an important force to appease and to be seen to appease (De La Bédoyère, 2015).

The blend within Brigantia is indeed numerous. Within her we have the mother and the warrior and we have a deity that bears the old world and the new world. Within her lies the ability to expand and subdivide, as she did as Brigit/Brigid/Maman Brigitte. Brigantia further proves the wheel or cycle of life, showing us how her energy force rotates, encompasses, gathers and becomes. From primordial mother goddess of Egypt and Gaul to military monarch of Rome and Greece, once more to earth mother goddess and then as Saint she is a continuous energy in motion. This continuous energy in motion is the reason that Brigid is such a unique deity.

Brigantia is the sovereign lady of the land. Her origins are found in the northern territories and have expanded across the British empire and overseas. The swan, one of her associated animals is the shape of the Isle of Avalon, one of the most sacred and spiritual territories in Britain. Brigantia as tribal goddess she could also be deemed the personification of earth. She is the name to call for healing, fertile and protective powers contained on earth. She is the healer through all her plants, herbs, crystals, flowers, minerals and animals. Her season of the year is autumn, when she has come into full ripeness in the second harvest. She is hard, dense matter as the earth, growing and expanding. First as goddess, then as territorial goddess (Brigantes), national goddess (Britannia) and into humanised saint form as Saint Brigid. It is she who calls us to ground into her body, the earth, to put down our roots where we are in the world and to release to her fear and anxiety in the root chakra. As earth mother, it is she who leads us to manifest and materialise all that we want when we activate our inner queen who is relentless in the hunt or pursuit of all that she desires. Her ability to create what she wants in her life comes from her maturity and from knowing who she is. It also comes from her clarity and healthy perspective. She is wild and free in herself and wild and free in her thinking. Therefore, no decision she makes gives a sense of entrapment. Like the eagle she has a bird's eye view and knows what course of action she takes comes from a sound place within her rather than fear-based decisions. With sceptre in hand, seated on her throne, crown straightened, she holds total dominion over her life. All that is not hers for the choosing needed to be eradicated. And with her choices, she accepts full accountability and full responsibility. Beholden to none, she is the sole ruler of her life.

Brigantia is the blend of the comforting, nurturing mother, and the wild protective mother. She is mother to her children and to her tribe. She takes action to sort it, whatever it may be. She puts herself on the line and calls it out as she sees it. Brigantia is authority. She asks us to honestly contemplate how we were taught to view power as a child and asks us to consider if that viewpoint is affecting our actions and life choices today. Once we view with compassion and understanding she asks us to heal our relationship to it, if it is in need of healing and in doing so, to step into our own divine power.

When I connect into her energy, I feel the colours blue and gold. Mostly I sense blue. I notice how this colour calms me, activates the throat chakra and it is the colour of the flame closest to source. It reminds me of her strength, that she is at the core of us all and thusly she reminds me of my own strength. When I am overwhelmed with images of wars and question what type of world I am living in, it is her name that I call to. I also call to her when I am worried about climate change. I recognise her in all those actively taking steps to save our planet. When I need a visual of her, I sense her as the wild spirit of the north on horseback flying into action or seated demure high on her throne, emanating sovereignty, full of wisdom and counsel.

In conclusion, we can view Brigantia as a mother goddess, war goddess, territorial goddess, healer and sovereign goddess of the Brigantes. She is connected to water and its healing properties. Brigantia is a classical conglomeration with personality traits identifiable with Jupiter, Caelestis and Minerva, more than likely evolving into Brigid through the Brigantes tribe. She, most like the Brigid I know, is open to change, forever evolving to suit the needs of all those who worship her. Brigantia is undeniably a goddess of unity in her ability to unite the Brigantian tribe. She may also represent unity between Ireland, Britain, Gaul and Celtic Hispania sharing the worship of a 'high exalted' goddess (Beck, 2009).

Out of all the titles we can give to Brigantia, I think the most fitting is warrior goddess. Out of a warring society she may have come into being, maybe brought in by the Gauls to Britain, who were themselves escaping Roman invasion. Under Roman rule in Britain, she rose in status. War surrounds her birth and her rise, and this is what I feel is what she is asking to be associated with in today's world. We cannot look back at the so-called savage Celtic society and think those days are gone. They are not. We are living with the constant threat of world war from this side of the world whilst two wars on the other side of the world rage on. Although we are not witnessing killings and bombings first hand from this privileged position, we are bombarded with news of war and its imagery everywhere. Brigantia's time has come back. Roman rule has ended but their influence on a Celtic deity remains. She is equipped and ready for action when called.

There has been a 'bringing her home' movement in Ireland to mark the 1500 anniversary of the death of Saint Brigid. I always find it interesting how the lives of saints are celebrated upon their deaths. The Goddess, as it were, is alive everywhere. Instead of reclaiming her as an historic figure and containing her in one place, could we recognise her blend and how she belongs nowhere specifically because she is everywhere. I suggest instead of bringing her home physically that we bring her home spiritually into our minds and hearts. As well as the bringer of the light we can see the depth of all that she is. She is the dark mother goddess Maman Brigitte and she is the sovereign war-goddess Brigantia. Recognising these integral parts of her as the divine feminine would really bring her home and help us awaken all traits of the goddess within us.

Throughout this journey of researching Brigantia I encountered many examples of triplism concerning Bri: Beck (2009) has a triplism of British Brigantia, Celtiberian Matres Brigiacae and Gaulish Brigindona. She argues these are etymologically related to the Irish goddess Brigit. The three Brigits; healer, poet and smithy. We can see triplism in Brigantia through Jupiter, Caelestis and Minerva. Jolliffe (1941) has her own triplism of Brigantia, Brigindu of Volnay and Brigid of Ireland. All these triplums indicate her impressive varied blended energy. This is what makes Brigid so remarkable. All her faces are incredibly unique, but they are all housed within the one Brigid. For me, my personal triune goddess comprises of Brigit, Maman Brigitte and now Brigantia. Brigit, Mother Goddess, Maman Brigitte, Dark Goddess and Brigantia, Warrior Goddess. Journey well with each aspect of Brigid and look forward to stepping into your sovereign-like energy with Brigantia. She is golden.

Bibliography

Adkins, L. and Adkins, R., 1996. *Dictionary of Roman religion.* Facts on File.

Akgoz, R., 2020. Roman Religion(2) Roman Religion | Riza Akgoz - Academia.edu

Aldhouse-Green, M., 2017. Women and goddesses in the Celtic world. In *Religion: Empirical Studies* (pp. 193-208). Routledge.

Anwyl, E. "Ancient Celtic Goddesses." *The Celtic Review*, vol. 3, no. 9, 1906, pp. 26–51. JSTOR, https://doi.org/10.2307/30069895. Accessed 4 Feb. 2024

Ballard, Robert. "HADRIAN'S WALL." *Teaching History*, vol. 3, no. 10, 1973, pp. 106–08. JSTOR,

Beck, N., 2009. *Goddesses in Celtic Religion: cult and mythology: a comparative study of ancient Ireland, Britain and Gaul* (Doctoral dissertation, Lyon 2).

Beck, N., theses.univ-lyon2.fr/documents/getpart.php?id=lyon2.2009.beck_n&part=159156

BENARIO, HERBERT W. "BOUDICA WARRIOR QUEEN." *The Classical Outlook*, vol. 84, no. 2, 2007, pp. 70–73. JSTOR, http://www.jstor.org/stable/43939202. Accessed 4 Jan. 2024.

Birnbaum, L.C., 2001. *Dark mother: African origins and godmothers.* iUniverse.

Bridgman, Timothy P. "Keltoi, Galatai, Galli: Were They All One People?" *Proceedings of the Harvard Celtic Colloquium*, vol. 24/25, 2004, pp. 155–62. JSTOR, http://www.jstor.org/stable/40285187. Accessed 8 Jan. 2024

Christoph M. Bulst. "The Revolt of Queen Boudicca in A.D. 60." *Historia: Zeitschrift Für Alte Geschichte*, vol. 10, no. 4, 1961, pp. 496–509. JSTOR, http://www.jstor.org/stable/4434717. Accessed 4 Jan. 2024.

Byrne, F.J., 1973. *Irish kings and high-kings.* Batsford.

Cohen, Paul, and Brenda Cohen. "The Roman Baths Museum In Bath, England." *Journal of College Science Teaching*, vol. 29, no. 4, 2000, pp. 285–86. JSTOR, http://www.jstor.org/stable/42990285. Accessed 21 Jan. 2024

Condren, M., 1989. *The serpent and the goddess: women, religion, and power in Celtic Ireland*. Harper & Row.

Cunliffe, B., 2013. *Britain begins*. Oxford University Press, USA.

Cunliffe, B.W., 1994. *Prehistoric Europe: an illustrated history*. *(No Title)*.

Cunliffe, B., 2018. *The ancient celts*. Oxford University Press.

de Jubainville, H. d'Arbois. "LE DIEU GAULOIS BELENUS LA DÉESSE GAULOISE BELISAMA." *Revue Archéologique*, vol. 25, 1873, pp. 197–202. JSTOR, http://www.jstor.org/stable/41736923. Accessed 19 Jan. 2024

De la Bédoyère, G., 2015. *The real lives of Roman Britain*. Yale University Press.

Ellis, P.B., 1994. *The Druids*. Constable.

Ellis, P.B., 1995. *Celtic women: women in Celtic society and literature*. *Constable and Company Ltd*.

Ellis, P.B., 2013. *A brief history of the Celts*. Hachette UK.

en.wikipedia.org/wiki/Cartimandua accessed 03/01/23 at 19.46

Fairless, K.J., 1989. *Aspects of the archaeology of the brigantes* (Doctoral dissertation, Durham University).

Gimbutas, M., 1974. *The gods and goddesses of old Europe: 7000 to 3500 BC myths, legends and cult images* (Vol. 4). Univ of California Press.

Gimbutas, M., 2001. *The living goddesses*. Univ of California Press.

Gimbutas, M., *The "Monstrous Venus" of Prehistory: Divine Creatrix in all Her Names*, (1991).

Graf, F., 2001. Athena and Minerva: two faces of one goddess? In *Athena in the Classical World* (pp. 127-139). Brill.

Green, M. ed., 2012. *The Celtic World*. Routledge.

Green, M., 2002. *Animals in Celtic life and myth*. Routledge.

Green, M., 1997. *Celtic Goddesses*. British Museum Press.

Bibliography

Green, M.A., 2011. *The gods of the Celts*. The History Press.

Hanson, W.S. and Campbell, D.B., 1986. The Brigantes: from clientage to conquest. *Britannia*, 17, pp.73-89.

Hathaway, S.L., 2021. The Figure of Minerva in Medieval Literature by William F. Hodapp. *Parergon, 38*(2), pp.223-224.

Henig, M.M. and Henig, M., 2003. *Religion in Roman Britain*. Routledge.

Hutton, R., 2013. *Pagan Britain*. Yale University Press.

J.F. Nagy, *Wisdom of the Outlaw*, Univ. Calif., 1985

James Mac Killop, *Dictionary of Celtic Mythology*, Oxford Univ Pr: 1998 Séamas Ó Catháin, *The Festival of Brigit*, DBA Publications, 1995; ISBN 0-9519-6922-6

Jerary, M. Tahar. "SEPTIMIUS SEVERUS THE ROMAN EMPEROR, 193-211 AD." *Africa: Rivista Trimestrale Di Studi e Documentazione Dell'Istituto Italiano per l'Africa e l'Oriente*, vol. 63, no. 2, 2008, pp. 173–85. JSTOR, http://www.jstor.org/stable/25734499. Accessed 27 Mar. 2024

Johnson, L.T., 2009. *Among the gentiles: Greco-Roman religion and Christianity*. Yale University Press.

Jolliffe, N., 1941. Dea Brigantia. *Archaeological Journal, 98*(1), pp.36-61.

Kajava, Mika. "Hestia Hearth, Goddess, and Cult." *Harvard Studies in Classical Philology*, vol. 102, 2004, pp. 1–20. JSTOR, https://doi.org/10.2307/4150030. Accessed 21 Jan. 2024.

Koch, J.T. and Cunliffe, B., 2012. Celtic from the West: alternative perspectives from archaeology, genetics, language and literature.

Leeming, D. and Fee, C., 2016. *The goddess: Myths of the great mother*. Reaktion Books.

MacCulloch, J.A., 2014. *Religion of the ancient celts*. Routledge.

MacMillan, C., 2007. The Feminine in the Culture of the Ancient Britons. *Gender Studies*, (06), pp.90-104.

McBurney, J., 2016. The Cult of Sulis-Minerva at Bath: The Religious Ritual of the Patron Goddess at Bath.

McGrath, S., https://earthandstarryheaven.com/2016/03/16/brigantia/

Miles, D., 2005. *The Tribes of Britain: Who Are We? And where do we come from.* Orionbooks

Murdock, M., 1990. *The Heroine's Journey: Woman's Quest for Wholeness.* Shambhala Publications.

Nelson, D.L., 1995. *The Indo-European origins of Minerva.* University of Pittsburgh.

Nicholson, F., 1999. Brighid: What Do We Really Know? *Celtic Well E-Journal.*

Njai, R., The Face of Britain before and after the Roman Invasion, 2013.

Ó Catháin, S., *The Festival of Brigit,* DBA Publications, 1995

Ó hÓgáin, D., 2002. The Celts: a history.

Ó hÓgáin, D., 2006. The lore of Ireland: an encyclopaedia of myth, legend and romance. *(No Title).*

Orpen, Goddard H. "Ptolemy's Map of Ireland." *The Journal of the Royal Society of Antiquaries of Ireland,* vol. 4, no. 2, 1894, pp. 115–28. JSTOR, http://www.jstor.org/stable/25508121. Accessed 18 Jan. 2024

Preston, J.J. ed., 2017. *Mother worship: Theme and variations.* UNC Press Books.

Roberts, A., 2015. *The Celts.* Heron Books.

Ross, Anne. *Pagan Celtic Britain,* Academy Chicago Pub, 1997

Ross, A., 1970. Everyday life of the pagan Celts. *(No Title).*

Russell, M. and Laycock, S., 2011. *UnRoman Britain: Exposing the great myth of Britannia.* The History Press.

Salway, P., 1965. *The frontier people of Roman Britain.* CUP Archive.

Sheridan, James J. "THE ALTAR OF VICTORY — PAGANISM'S LAST BATTLE." *L'Antiquité Classique,* vol. 35, no. 1, 1966, pp. 186–206. JSTOR, http://www.jstor.org/stable/41673351. Accessed 21 Jan. 2024

Bibliography

Stanier, Tom. "The Brigantes and the Ninth Legion." *Phoenix*, vol. 19, no. 4, 1965, pp. 305–13. *JSTOR*, https://doi.org/10.2307/1085830. Accessed 6 Jan. 2024

Stevens, C. E. "Hadrian and Hadrian's Wall." *Latomus*, vol. 14, no. 3, 1955, pp. 384–403. *JSTOR*, http://www.jstor.org/stable/41518029. Accessed 6 Jan. 2024.

Stone, C., 2019. Brigid or Brigantia: A 'Pan-Celtic' Goddess in Profile.

Strong, R., 2018. *The Story of Britain: From the Romans to the Present*. Hachette UK.

TIMES, I.P.C., ANWYL, E., WELSH, O. and AT, C.P., CELTIC RELIGION.1906, Archibald Constable and C0 LTD, Edinburgh.

W. J. W. *The Celtic Review*, vol. 10, no. 39, 1915, pp. 280–84. *JSTOR*, https://doi.org/10.2307/30070350. Accessed 19 Jan. 2024

Webster, J., 1995. Translation and subjection: interpretation and the Celtic Gods. *BAR INTERNATIONAL SERIES, 602*, pp.175-175.

Webster, J., 1995. Translation and subjection: interpretation and the Celtic Gods. *BAR INTERNATIONAL SERIES, 602*, pp.175-175.

Wright, R.E., 1995. *Vesta: a study on the origin of a goddess and her cultus*. University of Washington.

www.roman-britain.co.uk/tribes/brigantes accessed 13 Jan. 2024

Zoll, A.L., 1995. Patterns of worship in Roman Britain: double-named deities in context. *Theoretical Roman Archaeology Journal*, (1994).

About the Author

Pauline Breen is the author of three books on Brigid and is passionate about showing the various faces of the Goddess and Saint that she considers are often overlooked. In *This Is Brigid: Goddess & Saint of Ireland,* Pauline introduces Brigid in her original, pagan form as mother goddess and then as Christian saint. She considers both the goddess and the saint, shows the interplay between them and suggests ways to connect to Brigid through her symbols, numbers, animals and practices. In her second book, *Maman Brigitte: Dark Goddess of Africa and Ireland,* Pauline shows another lesser-known face of Brigid, a vodou deity that came into being during the hardship of slavery. Maman Brigitte is a blended deity from indigenous African deities and Brigid of Ireland. In her third book *Brigantia: Warrior Goddess*, she explores the idea that the migrating Brigantes tribes of northern England brought Brigid into Ireland, as we know her today.

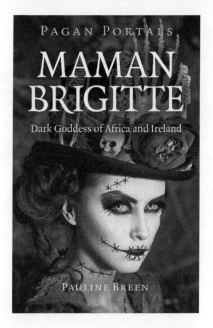

About the Author

Through research, fieldwork, and personal experience, the author uncovers the story of Brigitte in Haiti, Brigitte in Louisiana, and Brigitte today, a dark goddess in the contemporary world.

978-1-80341-736-3 (Paperback)
978-1-80341-735-6 (e-book)

MOON BOOKS
PAGANISM & SHAMANISM

What is Paganism? A religion, a spirituality, an alternative belief system, nature worship? You can find support for all these definitions (and many more) in dictionaries, encyclopaedias, and text books of religion, but subscribe to any one and the truth will evade you. Above all Paganism is a creative pursuit, an encounter with reality, an exploration of meaning and an expression of the soul. Druids, Heathens, Wiccans and others, all contribute their insights and literary riches to the Pagan tradition. Moon Books invites you to begin or to deepen your own encounter, right here, right now.

If you have enjoyed this book, why not tell other readers by posting a review on your preferred book site.

Bestsellers from Moon Books
Pagan Portals Series

The Morrigan
Meeting the Great Queens
Morgan Daimler

Ancient and enigmatic, the Morrigan reaches out to us. On shadowed wings and in raven's call, meet the ancient Irish goddess of war, battle, prophecy, death, sovereignty, and magic.
Paperback: 978-1-78279-833-0 ebook: 978-1-78279-834-7

The Awen Alone
Walking the Path of the Solitary Druid
Joanna van der Hoeven

An introductory guide for the solitary Druid, The Awen Alone will accompany you as you explore, and seek out your own place within the natural world.
Paperback: 978-1-78279-547-6 ebook: 978-1-78279-546-9

Moon Magic
Rachel Patterson

An introduction to working with the phases of the Moon, what they are and how to live in harmony with the lunar year and to utilise all the magical powers it provides.
Paperback: 978-1-78279-281-9 ebook: 978-1-78279-282-6

Hekate
A Devotional
Vivienne Moss

Hekate, Queen of Witches and the Shadow-Lands, haunts the pages of this devotional bringing magic and enchantment into your lives.
Paperback: 978-1-78535-161-7 ebook: 978-1-78535-162-4

Bestsellers from Moon Books

Keeping Her Keys
An Introduction to Hekate's Modern Witchcraft
Cyndi Brannen
Blending Hekate, witchcraft and personal development together to create a powerful new magickal perspective.
Paperback: 978-1-78904-075-3 ebook 978-1-78904-076-0

Journey to the Dark Goddess
How to Return to Your Soul
Jane Meredith
Discover the powerful secrets of the Dark Goddess and transform your depression, grief and pain into healing and integration.
Paperback: 978-1-84694-677-6 ebook: 978-1-78099-223-5

Shamanic Reiki
Expanded Ways of Working with Universal Life Force Energy
Llyn Roberts, Robert Levy
Shamanism and Reiki are each powerful ways of healing; together, their power multiplies. Shamanic Reiki introduces techniques to help healers and Reiki practitioners tap ancient healing wisdom.
Paperback: 978-1-84694-037-8 ebook: 978-1-84694-650-9

Southern Cunning
Folkloric Witchcraft in the American South
Aaron Oberon
Modern witchcraft with a Southern flair, this book is a journey through the folklore of the American South and a look at the power these stories hold for modern witches.
Paperback: 978-1-78904-196-5 ebook: 978-1-78904-197-2

Readers of ebooks can buy or view any of these bestsellers by clicking on the live link in the title. Most titles are published in paperback and as an ebook. Paperbacks are available in traditional bookshops. Both print and ebook formats are available online.

Find more titles and sign up to our readers' newsletter
www.collectiveinkbooks.com/paganism

For video content, author interviews and more, please subscribe to our YouTube channel.

MoonBooksPublishing

Follow us on social media for book news, promotions and more:

Facebook: Moon Books

Instagram: @MoonBooksCI

X: @MoonBooksCI

TikTok: @MoonBooksCI